THE WORLD OF HUNTING

THE WORLD OF
HUNTING

MERIEL BUXTON

·THE·
SPORTSMAN'S
PRESS
LONDON

Published by The Sportsman's Press 1991

For James

*A Catalogue record for this book
is available from the British Library*

ISBN 0–948253–53–3

Typeset, printed and bound in Great Britain by
Redwood Press Limited
Melksham, Wiltshire

CONTENTS

ACKNOWLEDGEMENTS

M y first and greatest debt of gratitude is to the forty-two brave people who agreed to be interviewed for inclusion in this book. Meeting them has been my greatest pleasure in the writing of this book. I feel that I have made some marvellous new friends, and only regret that my words can never do them justice. So often I have longed to share with the reader their voices and especially their smiles.

Many other people have helped me with advice and suggestions. In particular, I would like to thank the following: Miss Gloria Abbey, Mrs J. Aldridge, MFH, Miss E. Barker, Major Sir Rupert Buchanan-Jardine Bt, MC, MFH, Col the Hon. R. N. Crossley, TD, MFH, Mrs H. Gingell, MH, Mrs R. Peters, Major and Mrs A. G. Stewart, Sir John Thomson, Miss J. Walker-Okeover, MFH, Captain R. E. Wallace, MFH, Mrs M. C. Willes, MFH, Mrs Rachel Woollett and Messrs M. J. Barclay, MFH, A. Collins, J. Cowen, MFH, A. R. L. Escombe, N. M. L. Ewart, MFH, A. H. B. Hart, A. Jackson, T. R. P. S. Norton, MFH, R. W. F. Poole, MFH and N. C. Stirling, MFH.

For the illustrations, I would particularly like to thank Jim Meads for all his patient help; Lady Victoria Cuthbert for permission to use the picture by John King which illustrates Chapter 4 and John King himself for help in obtaining the print. I would also like to thank those responsible for providing the other photographs, whose names are given beside each print, and to offer my apologies to the photographers who took the pictures accompanying chapters 13 and 28 as I have been unable to identify them.

My family as always has been a tower of strength. My mother and brothers have made many constructive comments. My husband James has read, reread and advised upon every chapter, as well as taking many of the photographs. Rose and Hugh have offered unfailing support, and without Hugh's expertise on the word processor the manuscript would probably never have been completed.

Some of the Leading Figures in the World of Hunting

There are some two hundred different packs of foxhounds in England, Wales and Scotland and each has its own individual organisation, making it impossible to do more than generalise about the positions and roles of the various officials and helpers. As those included in this book come from hunting countries of every different type, no one man or woman can be truly representative of his or her counterparts throughout Britain: the role of the huntsman of one of the Shire packs, for example, is inevitably quite different from that of the huntsman in a small hill country, though there will also be much common ground. The notes below can only therefore give some general guidance.

The Master of Fox Hounds (MFH) may be a single individual, or, more frequently today, is one of two or more Joint Masters. He is responsible to the Committee for the organisation of the hunt and the employment of hunt staff. With very few exceptions, he is unpaid. Indeed, in the past he was generally given a guaranteed sum towards hunt expenses by the Hunt Committee and accepted responsibility for all expenditure beyond this figure. Whilst this still happens in a few countries, many Masters today contribute a known amount, sometimes substantial, but leave the Hunt Committee, and thus the subscribers, to carry the unlimited financial responsibility.

The Field Master   In countries where there is a large 'field' of mounted followers, a Field Master is appointed to be in charge of them during the day's hunting. He will lead the way and everyone is expected to obey him. He will usually, but not always, be one of the Masters.

The Professional Huntsman   His full time, paid job is to carry the horn and hunt, or control, hounds during the day's sport and to look after hounds in kennels.

Often, hounds are hunted by one of the Masters, who will be
The Amateur Huntsman   He is an unpaid person, usually one of the Masters, who carries the horn, hunting, or controlling, hounds in the hunting field. It is unusual, though by no means unknown, for an amateur also to look after hounds in kennels: generally a professional is employed for this purpose, called a Kennel Huntsman.

The Kennel Huntsman   In countries where there is an amateur huntsman, there is usually a professional kennel huntsman to perform the duties of the professional huntsman in kennels. He will generally 'whip in' (see below) to the amateur huntsman in the field, and carry the horn on any occasion when the amateur huntsman is unable to hunt hounds himself.

The Whipper-in is sometimes incorrectly referred to as 'the Whip'. A professional man or woman who acts as the huntsman's chief assistant on hunting days both by helping to control hounds, sending them back to the huntsman, and with information about the fox and in other ways. He also works with him in kennels to look after hounds and is normally responsible for the collection of the flesh (dead stock) from the farms.

   The whipper-in's job is traditionally regarded as a rung on the ladder towards becoming a professional huntsman. In the past many packs employed First and Second Whippers-in, but this is now extremely rare.

The Amateur Whipper   Many hunting countries today cannot afford to have two paid mounted members of staff in the hunting field. Every huntsman, professional or amateur, needs a whipper-in to 'turn' hounds to him and this is now done increasingly frequently by a competent, responsible member of the field hunting at his or her own expense. Even in countries with a professional whipper-in, there is often also an amateur giving support.

The Kennelman is a paid member of the hunt staff who does not come out hunting on a horse. He may assist or replace the whipper-in in kennels. He is usually responsible for the skinning and preparation of flesh collected from the farms for feeding hounds, and sometimes helps the whipper-in with the collection. He will also take responsibility for putting down old or injured horses and for the humane destruction of other animals at the request of their owners.

The Puppy Walker   Someone who volunteers, or is persuaded, free of charge, to take one or more hound puppies into his or her home and look after it or them from the time when the puppy is weaned until it is ready to return to kennels about six months later and join the pack.

The Hunt Secretary   Terms on which the Hunt Secretary operates vary enormously from country to country. Some are paid, some are honorary. In some countries there is just one, in others two or more work together. Some Hunt Secretaries are involved with the construction and repair of hunt fences, others are concerned only with financial and administrative matters. The most important duty common to all Hunt Secretaries is that of collecting subscriptions or 'caps' (payment for a single day's sport) from all those wishing to hunt. The Secretary is responsible to the Committee, not to the Masters.

The Farmer   Whether he hunts himself or not, he is the most important person in the hunting world. Without his hospitality in welcoming hounds and hunting people on to his land, the sport would cease.

The Fence Repairer   In some of the wealthier countries a fence repairer is employed on a full- or part-time basis to mend damage done during the day's hunting and to build new fences. He usually follows hounds in a Land Rover with his tools in the back, so that repairs to a farmer's damaged fencing are attended to soon after the damage happens.

Earth Stopper and Terrier Man   Some of the larger hunts employ an earth stopper and terrier man who is responsible for seeing that the earths are stopped before a day's hunting, but will not stop every earth personally. Men and occasionally women throughout the country are paid small amounts to stop the earths in their particular area when hounds are expected there. The terrier man is responsible for the terriers, which are usually his own property, producing them during the day's hunting if a fox is run to ground, perhaps in an undetected earth which has not been stopped or which has become unstopped during the night, probably by badgers. Terriers are then used either to 'bolt' the fox, when hounds are held well back from the hole and the fox given a good start before being hunted again, or, if the fox has been causing damage and the farmer wants it killed, it will be humanely destroyed. Often terriers are not used and the fox is left alone where he has run to ground.

Grooms   Yards where the horses for hunt staff are kept and the larger private hunter yards are generally in the charge of a Head Groom, who may be male or female. The old fashioned holder of such a position, generally male, was known as the Stud Groom. Other grooms will also usually be employed. The expression 'girl groom' can include any girl working in stables from the most junior to a Head Groom.

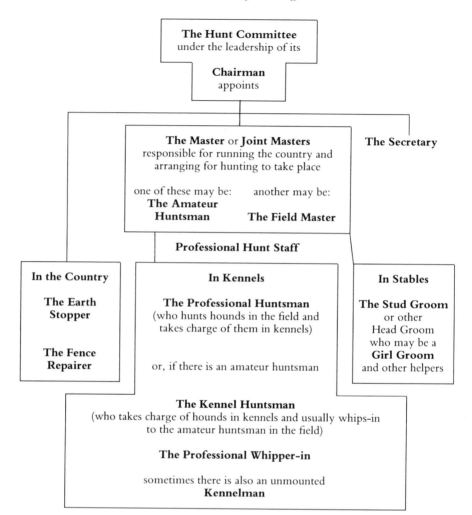

The Hunt Committee
under the leadership of its

Chairman
appoints

The Master or **Joint Masters**
responsible for running the country and
arranging for hunting to take place

one of these may be: another may be:
**The Amateur
Huntsman**   **The Field Master**

Professional Hunt Staff

In the Country

**The Earth
Stopper**

**The Fence
Repairer**

In Kennels

The Professional Huntsman
(who hunts hounds in the field and
takes charge of them in kennels)

or, if there is an amateur huntsman

In Stables

The Stud Groom
or other
Head Groom
who may be a
Girl Groom
and other helpers

The Secretary

The Kennel Huntsman
(who takes charge of hounds in kennels and usually whips-in
to the amateur huntsman in the field)

The Professional Whipper-in

sometimes there is also an unmounted
Kennelman

THE FIELD MASTER

Jim Bealby

'. . . remember you're leading
The cream of the cream in the shire of the shires.'

Bromley Davenport

Such is the privilege and also the responsibility of the Field Master of the Quorn in the Monday country. Jim Bealby has been fulfilling this role since 1985 and has won wide acclaim. Whilst he is only Field Master for one day a week (and an additional one Saturday in four), it is almost a full-time job throughout the hunting season. The Quorn Masters each take responsibility for the part of the country in which they act as Field Master. There are some 250 farmers in the Monday country; where a father and two sons are farming together, each of the three must receive equal consideration. A Monday is likely to affect between thirty and forty of them.

Many Masters send out postcards to farmers to tell them that hounds may cross their land on a particular date. Jim Bealby aims rather to speak to them all beforehand, actually visiting perhaps seventy per cent. He is reluctant to place the onus for contacting him on the farmer should some particular circumstance require special consideration: for example, ewes about to lamb in a certain field. He also personally gives the farmers on his list their point-to-point tickets, but does less summer visiting of farmers than some Masters deem necessary.

This constant visiting helps in many other ways. New plans for opening up different parts of the country may be discussed with farmers, and arrangements made for putting in new rails, or perhaps a bridge or wicket gate, or laying a hedge. The Quorn has an excellent back-up team to whom the Master can turn for actually doing the necessary work: the hunt spends over £40,000 a year on the country.

The knowledge thus gained is vital for the Field Master. Success on the day rests on two factors: knowing the country better than anyone and having horses to equal anyone else's. Jim Bealby considers he was fortunate when he first took on the job in finding 'three fabulous horses . . . they were all a bit screwy . . . not anyone's cup of tea but they jumped like stags and went like the wind.' He recollects an isolated refusal from one of them: a remarkable achievement over

Jim Bealby, MFH, leading the Quorn field with Mrs Di Hellyer. (*Jim Meads*)

Leicestershire fences when always going in front. Since he lost two of these horses, he feels that he has had 'a rough patch with some crashing falls.'

However good the horse, though, the duty of a Field Master is to lead his field, not jump some spectacular place where only a handful of others will follow. For it is vital to keep as many as possible of the field, which the Quorn struggles to keep below 160 in the Monday country, in contact with the Field Master. Most of the trouble is caused, not by the thrusters, but by the back-markers, up to an hour behind, taking a different route where they are not wanted or leaving gates open after the gate shutters have gone on.

Whilst the Master is appreciative that 'Quorn farmers have been brought up to see and expect huge fields over their land; many are great supporters and would not stop us under any conditions,' sometimes he has to disappoint his field when he knows that is right. Recently on such an occasion he held the gate open for the hunt staff then turned to the field: 'No-one through there.' Then he noticed the Prince of Wales: 'You can go, Sir, you can go.'

'Can I? Are you sure, Jim?' asked the Prince.

'Yes, hunt servants and princes of the realm.'

'In that order?' queried the Prince, laughing.

'Yes, in that order. No-one else: close the gate.'

Teamwork is essential. The Quorn have a tradition whereby Masters, Secretary, hunt staff and hounds unbox and hack on together. The fencing men and terrier men are also there. Thus plans can be finalised and information shared. Jim Bealby feels that his Joint Masters have been marvellous to work with, and that the three of them share the most important quality of all, a sense of humour.

The back-up team at home is equally important. A supportive, hunting wife and family make all the difference. Susan Bealby oversees the stables as well as the house and organises the paperwork on her computer, not to mention growing the best azaleas in the county. One of their sons takes full responsibility for the farming in winter. Without the family, although both Jim and Susan have always ridden, they might never have taken up hunting, for they only started when they saw what fun their children were having. Jim Bealby describes himself as 'of yeoman farming stock', the ideal background for enabling him to understand the farmers' point of view.

Controlling the field has proved easier than expected, thanks perhaps to good discipline from his predecessors. He has never so far had to send anyone home, though a bad scenting day in good country with a large, expectant field can be a nightmare. It amazes him that the field does not appreciate the need to give huntsman and hounds room. When having to wait, it would be much better to do so well back from the next fence, but pushing fields tend to make this impossible by engulfing the Field Master. It is always imperative to think well ahead for it takes time to stop the field, which is often best done with a hand in the air. Spoken orders must be loud and clear, but given without loss of temper, as, on a rare lapse, his son once quietly reminded him: 'Father, for heaven's sake: you're making an exhibition of yourself.' At such moments the Field Master has to recall that hunting is meant to be fun. His task is made easier with the Quorn since the huntsman Michael Farrin is such a superb horseman whom it is a privilege to follow.

Failure correctly to anticipate the way the fox will run may lead to the embarrassment of finding the whole field standing on the line. The thoughtful Field Master also considers the feelings of others in smaller matters, avoiding, for instance, flustering a young Whipper-in who has dismounted for a gate.

Jim Bealby summarises successful Field Mastership as a built up mutual trust between the mounted field and Field Master, with the field confident that they will get as good a ride as possible once hounds are running. The Quorn Monday field is well satisfied.

THE CAR FOLLOWER
Robert Blades

Robert Blades is an enthusiast. When asked which side of hunting most appeals to him, he replies: 'The 'orses, the 'ounds, the foxes and the chase – the lot!' All his holidays (he drives a lorry cleaning road drains) are spent either in following hounds in the car or at country fairs, local shows, in the hound tent at the Great Yorkshire Show or at the Middleton Puppy Show.

He has lived all his life in the Yorkshire town of Malton, son of a family uninterested in hunting, though his father and the Middleton huntsman share an enthusiasm for racing pigeons. On Boxing Day the Middleton hounds meet in Malton. 'When I was young, I went down into town to Boxing Day meet, before I got a car like . . .' It was a turning point in his life. Robert recalls his delight as he watched hounds running across the land behind his home, now the site of an industrial estate with the by-pass beyond.

It was some years before he was able to pursue his interest much further. As soon as he had a car of his own he started to follow hounds. He found everyone friendly and soon he was taking part in everything. 'I called up the 'unt kennels one night to give me a 'unt card: "There's all the events what we do. If you're interested pop in."' Today Robert feels that all his friends are hunting folk, including most of those at work. One colleague was at first quite uninterested, but Robert's enthusiasm is infectious: the man is now as devoted to the Sinnington as Robert is to the Middleton.

One particular friendship started twenty years ago when Robert first had his car. Jim Moore has been hunting all his life. He remembers happily setting out earth stopping at the age of twelve with a neighbour, his pleasure turning to terror as they entered the dark wood at midnight. An older man than Robert, he is now retired from his job emptying dustbins, but throughout his life has continued to follow hounds on foot or by motorbike. As soon as Robert spotted him, 'I says "Get in my car and have a ride round" and that was it'; the two have hunted together ever since, Jim benefitting from the transport and Robert, particularly in the early days, from the older man's experience and knowledge. Jim's wife occasionally complains of the amount of time he devotes to hunting: perhaps that is why Robert has remained unmarried. The younger man shows little interest in Jim's accounts of the days when cubhunting started at 5.30 a.m.

and thirty horses would come out from the hunt stables. But he respects Jim's opinions: despite his own enthusiasm for terrier work, he concedes that, when a fox has given a good run, they should not dig it out, adding only, with wisdom, that this must depend on the landowner's wishes.

Unlike Jim, Robert has never ridden, though 'Folks keep nagging at me to have a go.' No doubt he will do so, but would probably be better suited could he ever exchange his car for a Land Rover. For the present, it is fortunate that he always takes out a full car load of supporters, for there are plenty of people to push when he gets stuck. Yet, unlike so many of those who used to ride but now follow hounds in the car, he does not seem frustrated by the limitations of a vehicle. On the contrary, he points out that he is occasionally able to get to hounds when those on horses are held up, though he is always careful not to head a fox.

Robert and his friends have a very different attitude from those car followers who have made themselves unpopular with many Masters and other hunting

Robert Blades (*right*) and Jim Moore. (*James Buxton*)

people. Too many of those in vehicles adopt the passive role of audience, determined to see as much as they can, regardless of the overall effect on the day's sport, participating only by an inappropriate holloa, too often right in the fox's face, intent on their own comfort, amusement and probably their lunch, and eager, as soon as the day is over, to hurry back to fireside or pub.

Robert and Jim take pride in playing an active role, always ready to find ways in which they can help. CB radio allows them to pass messages and information fast, and Robert frequently gives lifts or moves horseboxes, his HGV licence standing him in good stead. In summer too he willingly becomes a car park attendant at the point-to-point or moves show jumps for a fund raising event.

One day in every season is uniquely his own. He has his own lawn meet, not at his home in the town, but from the boot of his car. Some years ago he learnt that a particular fixture was habitually a dry occasion, and volunteered to offer hospitality. Now an unalterable annual event, his generosity is much appreciated by all.

Even on working days, occasionally his lunch break allows a quick sight of hounds, the big yellow vehicle attracting many friendly waves. Whilst essentially a Middleton man, Robert has hunted with most of the local packs, beagles as well as foxhounds. He was only sorry when the Middleton hounds recently had invitation days in both the Burton and the Wynnstay countries that time prevented him from going. He is determined to accept an invitation to the Brocklesby now that his friend Tony Edwards, the Middleton huntsman, is moving there.

Hunting for Robert Blades is more than a sport. It is a way of life in which he has found interest, enjoyment, social life and friends. He strives to put into it as much as he takes out, and has succeeded in making himself a special part of the establishment, a position he fully appreciates. Such car followers as Robert and Jim are never mere spectators.

3

THE PROFESSIONAL HUNTSMAN
Don Claxton

Don Claxton is a professional huntsman of the old school. Brought up in the Hurworth country in North Yorkshire, he helped his grandfather to break in young horses and soon shared the old man's enthusiasm for hunting. The Second World War gave him the chance to whip in to Ted Littleworth, the Hurworth huntsman, and he knew then that he wished to go into Hunt service. His first job was second horseman to Captain MacAndrew, Master of the Zetland, and the following season he became second whipper-in. He then moved to the Badsworth, the North Northumberland and the Middleton, where he was first whipper-in, before hunting the Atherstone in 1960. He moved to Alnwick to hunt the Percy Hounds in 1965, and has remained there ever since.

A career structure such as this, with successive promotions brought about by personal recommendations from the Masters he served, gave him a breadth of experience which is denied the young man entering the profession today. There are virtually no openings for second horsemen or second whippers-in. Promotion is swifter, but Don Claxton learnt much from the different men he worked under. Some were severe taskmasters, though none was quite so abrupt as the legendary Frank Freeman of the Pytchley. His nephew, George Gillson, later himself a great huntsman, arrived to whip in to him and knocked at the door. Freeman opened it a crack. 'Hound exercise six in the morning,' he barked, and shut the door.

Don Claxton enjoyed his time at the Atherstone, and found it an interesting country to ride across. When he first arrived, he asked three young boys to show him the way across the part before them. 'Yes, Sir!' they replied, grinning, and jumped three gates without a pause. The Atherstone at this time were hunting four days a week, with the Master carrying the horn on two of those days and the huntsman on the other two. The same system was followed with the Percy, when Don Claxton first moved there. The late Duke of Northumberland was Master of the Percy Hounds from 1940 until his death in 1988. He opened up the country so effectively that even today more fences are jumped than were before the War, although inevitably there is now considerably more plough. Occasionally this can lead to problems where hunt jumps are in the middle of fences dividing what used to be grass fields: new hunt jumps today are put in the corners of fields. The Percy country is mostly farmland with timber fences and relatively little moorland or woodland for Northumberland. The farmers are marvellously hospitable to hounds.

Kennels and stables are run to the same high standard as the rest of the Alnwick estate. When Don Claxton first arrived, there were two whippers-in and a kennelman as well as himself, and he did not then whip in on the days when the Duke was hunting hounds, although he was provided with two horses to hunt on those days. Later, following an outbreak of 'flu, the Duke found that he preferred to have him whipping in. The Duke was himself a superb hunts-man with a natural affinity with hounds, who had only to hear his voice to jump up enthusiastically, even though he might not see them from the end of the season until the Puppy Show. His many commitments meant that he had sometimes to spend four nights in a week on the sleeper to enable him to hunt hounds on two days.

The true huntsman is totally dedicated. Not only is he concentrating hard throughout the day, on hounds and how they are working, and on the fox and his likely reactions, but afterwards, at night, he thinks about what he has done wrong. Many factors, and bad scent in particular, may cause a succession of bad days. Once the Duke had a series of such days, whilst all the good hunts seemed to be when Don Claxton was hunting hounds. The huntsman, worried, said 'You must think I'm feeding your hounds different to mine.' The Duke was unconcerned. 'What's wrong with the hounds?' he demanded. 'They're trying. It's when they're not trying that there is something to worry about.' Sure enough, soon afterwards fortunes were reversed and it was Don's turn for a run of bad days.

Many theories have been put forward as to what makes a good or bad scenting day. A lifetime's experience has convinced Don Claxton that none of these can be relied on and, until a fox is found, scenting conditions cannot be accurately predicted. There is even considerable variation between one fox and another; sometimes the first indication the huntsman has that hounds have changed foxes comes from a marked deterioration in scent, or perhaps, if they were a long way behind and a fresh one has jumped up just in front of them, a conspicuous improvement. Fumes from vehicles impair scent, and grass fields bare from intensive grazing carry less scent than ploughed land.

In the Percy country, many of the earths are enormous and digging a fox out is not feasible. Don Claxton has no regrets about this, unless a farmer has particularly asked for a fox to be killed. 'I'm not a digging man', he says, his only concern being that hounds should mark properly and not be taken away from the earth too fast.

A disciplined field, brought up to hunt, helps the huntsman, and time spent explaining hunting to Pony Club members is worthwhile. The importance of pulling up as soon as hounds check is emphasised: galloping past at such a juncture is disastrous. Learning to do things the right way from an early age makes a difference: one of the best whippers-in Don ever had was his own son,

Don Claxton with the Percy Hounds in front of Alnwick Castle. (*Jim Meads*)

though neither of his sons is now in hunt service. For a huntsman to show first rate sport, as Don Claxton has done in the Percy country for more than a quarter of a century, he needs the right team behind him, in the stables as well as the kennels. At Alnwick this was provided for more than forty years by Fred Litster, the subject of the next chapter.

4

THE STUD GROOM
Fred Litster

'Never forget, your fences are jumped in the stable, and your foxes are killed in kennels,' an old man told Fred Litster when he started work with hunters. The boy thought he was joking until the old man explained 'If they are not looked after inside, they won't do their work outside.' It is advice which he has never forgotten, in a career lasting sixty-three years.

Fred Litster's father, grandfather and great uncle had all been with horses and he never doubted that that was where his future lay. His first job was in 1926, in Lord Joicey's yard. The stud groom, a former sergeant-major called Cotton, not only gave him a thorough training but imbued him with his own impeccable standards. Ten years later he went to Captain Hall Watt as second whipper-in, but this never appealed to him as did his work with horses. Soon he laid aside his red coat and returned to the stables.

During the War, he was with the Durham Light Infantry, serving in the front line in Burma, then in 1946, he came to work for the Duke of Northumberland at Alnwick, and was soon promoted to the position of stud groom. He remained there until 1989, when the amputation of a leg forced him to retire.

Fred Litster's long association with the Percy family has been a singularly happy one. Alnwick is an exceptional place in which to work and do horses. When he first arrived, there were some sixteen hunters, as well as brood mares and a stallion. One of his few unrealised ambitions was to win the Premium Stallion Championship, though Solon Morn was Reserve.

The magnificent stable yard adjoining the castle was then made up of stalls. Under Fred's auspices, these were converted to loose boxes, retaining all the superbly made old fittings, and the loose school adapted into an ideal exercising ground for frosty days. Outside, few yards in England can have more glorious country in which to exercise, nor conditions more ideal for fittening horses. The park, splendid in its variety and always beautiful, rises up past a tower built to repel northern invaders, from which seven castles may be seen. The long, upward sloping track ensures that any horse exercising that way regularly will soon be incomparably fit.

Proper fitness was always the stud groom's first priority. This must never be rushed, and any attempt at short cuts carries an increased risk of injury. The

(l. to r.) The Duchess of Northumberland, her daughter Lady Victoria Cuthbert, Fred Litster holding the grey horse, the 10th Duke of Northumberland, MFH, and huntsman Don Claxton, painted by John King. (*Photo A. C. Cooper Ltd. Reproduced by kind permission of Lady Victoria Cuthbert*)

hunters would come in in July, and for six weeks they walked for two hours a day, and never went out of a walk. After that they were worked at a steady six miles an hour hound jog, with as much hill work as possible. Great care was taken in the early days particularly to ensure that the saddle could not slip, for girth galls are caused by friction. The long hacks frequent before horse boxes kept horses in excellent condition.

He attaches less importance to the amount of strapping required, believing that 'the best groom is the bucket'. Individual attention to feeding is all-important: 'You can have fifty horses and not one will feed the same.' The Percy hunters in full work always had four feeds a day, the first at 5.30 a.m., the last at 9.30 or 10 at night. Whilst Fred Litster expected his staff to be disciplined and work hard, he demanded much more of himself. The staff would not enter the yard until 6.30 a.m. and everyone else had gone by 6 p.m., so both the early and late feeds were given by him, when the horses could eat in peace. Enjoyment is spoilt, as he says, if 'you're sitting down for a nice meal and someone comes along with a Hoover: whilst a common horse may stand it a well bred one will

not.' The groom must always notice, too, exactly what a horse has left un-
touched. A choosy feeder will often enjoy boiled swedes.

He never used haynets, preferring to feed naturally on the ground. This is not
a wasteful system provided that only a little is fed at a time and the groom keeps
going back. Many horses like to take a mouthful of hay and dip it in the water
'like an old girl with a biscuit in her tea'; they cannot do this with a haynet.
Whilst he used always to use wheat straw, long, not combined, which would be
plaited along the edge of the box, today he favours shavings, for the sprays used
on modern straw may cause coughing.

Many of the old remedies or their ingredients can no longer be obtained.
Aconite powders, for example, are no longer sold. Others were made from
herbs picked wild, which have also disappeared. Fred Litster's treatment for leg
problems remains easily available though: hot and cold water alternately, ban-
daging the cold hose to the leg, then applying heat through a kaolin poultice.
Soundness problems are not always easily diagnosed: 'My father used to say
"take the shoe off if his neck is broken." That seems Irish, but nine times out of
ten it's in the foot.'

One old-fashioned treatment he has never believed in is the administration of
a large quantity of physic when horses first come in. They would eat nothing for
a week afterwards: he considered it 'a lazy man's way of getting some meat off.'

After hunting, he would first see a horse stale, then allow him to roll if he
wished. He would give him a linseed gruel and mash, properly simmered for at
least four hours, and, whilst doing him, keep his ears dry. 'Keep them warm,
that's the secret,' he says. Feet are all picked out from the nearside, in the correct
order: off fore, near fore, off hind, near hind. When feeling a leg for heat or
filling, the good leg is always felt first. Dandy brushes are only used on the mane
and tail: many well bred horses will not tolerate them elsewhere.

Most of the Percy hunt horses, and the late Duke's own hunters, came from
Bert Cleminson in Yorkshire, who excelled at finding quality, weight carrying,
made hunters. The chestnut horse ridden by Don Claxton in John King's
picture, though, was not one of Cleminson's. He arrived in poor condition, but
under Fred's care he built up magnificently and proved 'a fantastic horse'. He is
still carrying the huntsman after more than seven seasons. One aspect of that
picture annoys Fred, who is always firm but gentle with his horses, constantly
talking to them: he was in fact painted separately from the horse he is holding,
and the horse is shown with its ears back: 'He thinks I'm going to hit him!' No
horse who knew Fred Litster well has ever looked at him like that: the Percy
horses, as well as the Master and hunt staff, appreciated their stud groom.

5

THE MASTER OF FOX HOUNDS
Captain Charles Barclay

'**O**f all sitivations under the sun, none is more enviable or more 'onerable than that of a master of fox'ounds!' declared Jorrocks, but, as Trollope pointed out, 'There are heavy duties, deep responsibilities, and much true heart-felt anxiety to stand as make-weight against all these sweets.'

Captain Charlie Barclay has been a Master of the Puckeridge, or Puckeridge and Thurlow, since 1947. During that time he has numbered amongst his Joint Masters his grandfather, father, wife, son and daughter. The sense of continuity thus created is an important element in the Puckeridge which extends beyond the Barclay family: there have only been six huntsmen since 1896, and the Master and most of the farmers have known each other all their lives. Perhaps this, combined with Captain Barclay's own considerable charm, is why he finds them as a group 'Fantastic – very co-operative', although in the last century Puckeridge farmers were notoriously awkward.

A nucleus of the farmers hunt, and some are very keen. Towards the end of each season there is a Farmers' Meet when some sixty or seventy farmers come out, and no-one else. As well as the regular hunting farmers, there are many others, some of whom virtually do not otherwise ride. Children's ponies, cobs and old stalwart horses are commandeered from every corner, a cap is taken for some deserving local cause and the day is rounded off with a supper party in the Master's house produced by the Supporters' Club, with a raffle to help towards costs. No doubt the caricatures on the walls of former Puckeridge subscribers inspire many modern comparisons, if there is no chance to appreciate the Master's collection of hunting books. Even when Captain Barclay missed virtually a whole season's hunting after breaking his leg, he managed to live up to expectations by hunting on that one day.

His first experience of whipping in was not with the Puckeridge but the Eton Beagles; 1937–8 was a vintage season: hounds killed 75½ brace of hares and three foxes. The huntsman's name was Ronnie Wallace. The whipper-in recalls that he 'soon realised how much there was to be learnt about hunting. Barclays have a habit of thinking they know it all, and one quickly realised one was pretty incompetent. I also made the mistake of thinking I liked and could play football, which (Ronnie Wallace) thought was a frivolous entertainment. How right he was . . .'

For Captain Barclay, the most important part of his Mastership has been hunting hounds himself. When he first joined his father and grandfather in the Mastership, his father handed over the horn to him, but continued to control the breeding policy for the rest of his life, and was the most powerful influence on Captain Barclay's own approach. The Puckeridge hounds have been shown successfully for many years, although the family has always had its priorities quite clear: showing is only a secondary amusement. Successive generations have also been ready to listen to new lines of thought whilst retaining the benefit of past experience. Captain Barclay's father's approach differed considerably from that of his grandfather. His father, towards the end of his life, began to appreciate the limitations of the Old English lines and feel the need to introduce fresh blood into the kennel; indeed in the last conversation he had with Captain Barclay he said that something must be done. Both men were much interested in the work of Sir Alfred Goodson.

Other hound breeders who have influenced Captain Barclay include the 10th

Captain Charles Barclay, MFH, casting the Puckeridge Hounds across arable land.
(*Jim Meads*)

Duke of Beaufort, of whom he says 'Everything with him took on extra added excitement and he was a wonderful man with hounds and dogs.' Sir Peter Farquhar Captain Barclay knew as 'a very fine, brave and kind gentleman whom one could not fail to admire, whose breeding of hounds was always a source of admiration and spirited debate in the Barclay family.' Another successful hound breeder and friend was Tony Cowen of the Braes of Derwent, like Charlie Barclay himself a countryman, naturalist and Master of Hounds.

The Puckeridge Hounds are proof that his breeding policy works. Not only do they show exceptional sport but, since the War, at Peterborough they have won three Championships and two Reserve Championships. The two recent champions, Pigeon in 1984 and Devious in 1989, have both proved outstanding successes in the field as well as on the flags, though Pigeon was killed by a car after a tragically short life.

Cars are just one of the modern hazards to affect hunting, and country life in general in this part of England. The kennels are only 35 miles from Marble Arch. Modern agricultural trends make it increasingly difficult to show sport in East Anglia, as intensive arable growing means that more and more of the country is ploughed up, with winter wheat everywhere, fences disappearing and the acres of stubble fields so characteristic of cubhunting in the past going under the plough immediately the combine harvester has done its job.

Many of the big landowners and their families are more interested in shooting than hunting. Captain Barclay regrets all this, for 'hounds and the English countryside are the reasons why I go hunting'.

He is personally less concerned by the effects of these changes on the riding side of hunting. Whilst his daughter and Joint Master, Mrs Pyper, is an outstanding horsewoman and cross-country rider, Captain Barclay describes himself as a 'doggy sort of man' who has always rated hounds a long way in front of horses. He enjoys spending as much time as he can in kennels with hounds: despite the merger with the Newmarket and Thurlow in 1970 two packs of hounds are now retained with separate kennels, each hunting their own parts of the country. The Puckeridge kennels, close to the Master's home, were rebuilt by the Supporters' Club.

The calls on a Master's time are endless, and he is ultimately responsible for so much, overseeing with his Joint Masters hounds, horses, the country, the hunt staff, earth stopping and so on, as well as attending numerous hunt functions. But Captain Barclay sees it all as part of his natural way of life. He enjoys knowing everyone, as everyone knows him, but regards this as one of the most important aspects of Mastership. 'Knowing what's going on' takes time and trouble, even for someone as much a part of his country as Captain Barclay. But 'you have the unique privilege of knowing Great Britain from the back of a horse, in all its moods and changing seasons.'

6

THE AMATEUR WHIPPER-IN
Maurice Eynon

Maurice Eynon has been whipping in to the South Pembrokeshire Hounds for some twenty seasons. Unlike most amateurs, he knows every hound by name. Farming as he does just two minutes' drive from the kennels, he regularly walks out with hounds and gets his own horses fit on hound exercise.

Despite having been a keen hunting man all his life, he did not start riding until after the births of both his children, Rachel and Richard. Mrs Eynon had always ridden and when Richard was eighteen months old she bought herself a horse which her husband exercised occasionally, and soon took out with hounds. Finding that on a horse he could be that much closer to hounds, able to sit and watch them work, he has never looked back.

Whipping in regularly as he does is a considerable commitment for himself and the rest of his family. The South Pembrokeshire hunt five days a fortnight. Maurice Eynon ensures that he is out every day, until hounds go home. With a 400 acre farm, a flock of 600 breeding ewes, 80 cows in milk and, apart from himself and Richard, only casual and contract labour, this requires hard work and a real team effort from the family. His wife and Rachel both hunt, and they do the horses, though Maurice sometimes helps with the clipping. Rachel has a part-time job milk recording for the Milk Marketing Board. In summer she works at the local Leisure Park. Richard also enjoys his hunting, though he does not ride. He does much of the terrier work for the South Pembrokeshire, using his sister's Borders.

Maurice Eynon also used to do a great deal with the terriers. The fifth generation of his family to farm their land, high above the West coast of Wales, he hunted regularly on foot for years before he started riding and probably knows the South Pembrokeshire country better than anyone else. When Simon Hart arrived as Master in 1988, he found him invaluable, not only as a whipper-in, particularly when the kennel huntsman was laid up following an operation, but for his help in getting to know the country and the farmers. The farmers also appreciate having one of their number up with hounds: sheep can be caught in briars and pop out suddenly right in front of hounds. If the whipper-in can anticipate such problems and free the sheep before hounds come up, it makes all the difference, although the South Pembrokeshire are very

Maurice Eynon, amateur whipper-in to the South Pembrokeshire Hounds,
with (*left*) Barry Summons. (*Jim Meads*)

steady. With gates to dismount for and low branches common, he prefers a
horse to be under 16 hands and sensible. 'Many times I've got to jump off
quickly and I just drop the reins.'

The Eynon family has been fortunate with horses, some cleverly chosen,
without any previous information, at Leicester sales. They like to buy made
hunters for themselves, but have been remarkably successful at breeding big,
quality horses on the farm to sell on as three-year-olds. Seabrook, one of the
outstanding heavyweight show hunters of the eighties, was bred here. The
Eynon family won some 26 championships with him in hand before sending
him to Malvern Sales as a three-year-old, where he fetched £7,000. Whilst he
was a horse in a lifetime, his dam produced eight foals in ten years, 'all good big

ones.' The farm is on limestone, which, the owner says modestly, is why 'all the
young ones do so well; it really makes the bone of them.' He combines this
natural advantage with considerable skill in both selection and feeding.

Maurice Eynon voluntarily takes on many of the duties of a professional
whipper-in away from the hunting field, helping with hound exercise, bringing
in flesh, helping to show hounds at Builth Wells Hound Show, and parading
them in the ring at other shows. He walks a puppy and will combine a few days'
hunting on Exmoor with taking a bitch to a stallion hound there: Captain
Wallace, with Major Gundry, has judged at the puppy show for many years,
and the help and guidance he has given the South Pembrokeshire has been
invaluable. Maurice Eynon helps the Master put in new gates and rails, he and a
neighbour spend two days each year building a fence for the point-to-point,
and, on the day, he is the starter whilst his wife sells the race cards. There is no
hunt horse box: the Eynon family drive hounds and the hunt horses in their own
lorry.

On hunting days they start at 5.30, father and son doing the milking and other
farm work, and mother and daughter doing horses and household chores. They
like to be ready by nine for breakfast and to sit down for twenty minutes, but
seldom finish in the evenings before eight. High standards are maintained –
manes and tails are always plaited – but all the family are fast workers and
modern techniques are used. The cows are fed on a computer system.

When hounds meet at his own farm, Maurice Eynon puts rails and gorse
across the gateways, enabling the field to have some jumping and keeping the
sheep in their fields without the need for shutting gates. His land is well foxed
and it is usually a good day. He himself is always alert, counting hounds,
thinking ahead and going on where necessary to prevent sheep springing up in
front of the pack or hounds getting into trouble on a main road, knowing where
foxes are likely to be lying and the quickest way to ride across the country. He
has taught his family much of this: Rachel will often slip on to the Master with
information. 'You've got to be watching all the time; you can't take your eyes
off. It's just scanning the country. It's surprising what you can see,' he says. This
is what makes him such a good amateur whipper-in: perhaps it is also why he
enjoys his hunting so much.

THE HUNT SUPPORTER
Mrs Clarrie Blackwell

Hunts throughout Britain have always had their supporters, many of whom never rode to hounds, but the idea of the Hunt Supporters' Club is a comparatively new one. The constant need for fund raising has been harnessed, very successfully in most countries, to the wish of those interested in hunting with a particular pack of hounds to help their chosen hunt. The resulting club organises numerous money-raising events throughout the year, most of which are also popular social functions. The money thus raised is spent for the benefit of the hunt, but the way in which it is used is at the discretion of the Supporters' Club Committee.

Whilst most Supporters' Clubs have many riding members, this is an area in which the non-riding car or foot follower comes to the fore. The initial reluctance in some countries to see such clubs established, born of concern lest the members should seek to control rather than merely support the hunt, has been proved groundless in the vast majority of cases. The magnificent gifts presented to hunts by their Supporters' Clubs have overwhelmed Masters and Hunt Committees everywhere, and would now be sorely missed.

As with every sort of human organisation, there are usually a few people who do all the work. The Grafton Hunt Supporters are fortunate: they have an excellent team of hard workers. Pre-eminent amongst them is Mrs Clarrie Blackwell. She has been on the Committee for more than a quarter of a century, although she had never been interested in hunting until one day, when their daughter was small, her husband suggested that they should go out with hounds for a little while. Soon she found herself so fascinated that the need to leave to meet her daughter from school caused considerable irritation. Now that she is semi-retired, she is able to hunt three days a week and work on the remaining three. Her husband, although less keen, generally accompanies her, for 'What else can you do in the winter really, in the country, apart from hunting?' she asks, and, on the days when Northampton Town is not playing, he agrees. As well as the Grafton, they frequently go out with the Bicester, Pytchley and Warwickshire, and have an occasional day with the Beaufort and elsewhere.

The Supporters' Club organises a succession of events throughout the year. The Harvest Supper is followed by a Cheese and Wine, the Christmas party, the Foxtrotters (a popular dance), an Open Day at the kennels, and many other

Mrs Clarrie Blackwell. (*Meriel Buxton*)

functions. There are also Skittles Evenings and Clay Pigeon shoots. With the exception of the latter, Mrs Blackwell is involved in almost everything. Where catering is done by the Committee, she will make mince pies or other delicacies beforehand, but on the day she is almost always on the door or gate, collecting money. She personally organises the annual trip to the Horse of the Year Show, booking and paying for a 53-seater bus in July and worrying that not enough people will want to come, needlessly, for there is always a waiting list.

She has a natural flair for salesmanship and combines this with dedication and determined hard work. All these qualities are needed in her collection of car caps. This is generally regarded as a thankless job, but Clarrie Blackwell has made a remarkable success of it, perhaps because she enjoys doing it. Apart from a few pensioners, who pay a single sum for the season, she goes round every car on every day's hunting with her bag, asking for donations. If she is hunting with one of the neighbouring packs, she still tries to attend the Grafton meet for this purpose. The friendly spirit in which she undertakes her task engenders good will and brings in substantial sums. Often too, she interests newcomers in joining the Supporters' Club, or collects subscriptions from existing members. She has recently instigated the production of a new Supporters' Club badge, sales of which make a further contribution. She herself collects the badges of Supporters' Clubs throughout Britain.

The Grafton Supporters' Club has recently bought, in the same year, a new knacker wagon and a ride-on lawn mower for the kennels, followed a year later by an investment of £8,000 in improvements to a house to be occupied by the new stud groom. Members also formed a team to do further work on the house. Mrs Blackwell has never accepted office within the Supporters' Club, but her work as a Committee member, or, as she describes herself, 'only an ordinary car follower', has indeed supported hunting in the Grafton country.

THE FENCE REPAIRER

Neil Seaton

Neil Seaton had no interest in hunting when he was asked by the Masters of the Meynell if he would do some fence repairs to help them out over the coming fortnight. Thirty-five years later he is not only responsible for mending every fence broken by the Meynell field but knows every farmer in the country and is the friend of most. He was advised early in his career always to consider that he worked for the farmers, and this has remained a guiding principle.

Neil has a small farm himself, with a herd of pedigree Holstein cattle and a flock of sheep, not to mention dogs, geese and white cats. His sympathy with the farmer's point of view would make him a good ambassador even without his natural abilities. He also has such a likeable manner, and such a twinkle, that anyone who can persist in his ill-humour after ten minutes with Neil must be obdurate indeed.

He is a great talker: he tells with delight how one incoming Master laughingly complained that taking on the Meynell Hounds, and Neil with them, was like buying a house with a gramophone which could not be switched off. His stories, often at the Masters' expense, are endless. Once, he says, he accompanied a new Master, elated with self-importance, on a visit to a farmer. They found the man busy grinding corn and unaware at first of their presence. The farmer suddenly saw them, jumped and exclaimed 'Oh, my God!'

Neil maintains that the Master replied 'No, no. It'll be all right; you can still call me by my Christian name.' But, as he says, 'I always start off on the truth but then I get carried away.'

Whilst an official fence repairer is now an accepted part of many hunts, this has not always been the case. In the nineteenth and early twentieth century, although farmers were recompensed for damage to livestock allegedly caused by foxes, a system open to widespread abuse, broken fences were not necessarily repaired. However in many countries there would be a man in every village who could be called upon to mend gaps or take down wire in his parish.

Neil's contract with the Meynell gives him greater freedom than other hunt fence repairers. The hunt pays for his vehicle and the timber he uses, though he selects and orders the timber himself, and he is expected to repair every gap made by those hunting. If he is asked to put in a new bridge or hand gate he is

Neil Seaton and his wife with HRH The Prince of Wales. (*Jim Meads*)

paid extra, but he will sometimes on his own initiative agree a new way across a farm with the farmer in order to minimise damage. He works with his son and enjoys his work: 'I like fencing and obviously I like talking and I've an awful lot of friends.'

In cases of trouble, he says 'If I can get there first I can always make it easier for the Masters.' He gives the farmers a chance to get rid of their anger, and, whilst he is happy to give reasons, he is not prepared to make excuses for the bad behaviour of hunting people, often agreeing that they are 'hooligans on horses'. He feels that relations between the hunting and farming communities have deteriorated in recent years because there is less mutual respect and understanding. Much ill-feeling can stem from a few minutes' thoughtlessness. One farmer's daughter had her car kicked and damaged by a horse. Surrounding horses prevented her from getting out and no apology was made. Another farmer's wife was made late for the children's school by a side ramp down across the road which the owner refused to move. Neil considers that in the past such inconsiderate behaviour would not have been tolerated by other members of the field. Today no-one wants to get involved. Episodes such as these can lead to trouble: 'It was always arrogance and ignorance that had got us warned off.' On the other hand, to Neil's pleasure, the current Mastership has won back the respect of the district.

The hunt is often made a scapegoat by farmers troubled by different problems. Where two brothers farming together were fighting between themselves there was always friction over hunting. When each acquired a separate farm all the problems ceased.

A telephone call can clear the air. Neil's wife often succeeds in calming an angry farmer with her soothing replies. Neil himself answered one smallholder complaining that he had had some sheep cast. 'Did you actually see hounds in the sheep?' asked Neil. 'No? Well, could it be that they didn't do it?'

'Were you with them all day?' demanded the farmer indignantly.

'No, to tell you the truth I wasn't with them at all,' admitted Neil. 'They did not hunt that day with the frost.'

Farmers occasionally own to some disappointment when a 'ratchety lot of fencing' survives a day's hunting unscathed: some strong new double-topped rails would have been most acceptable. Others generously offer to pay where Neil turns a gap made by cattle, not horses, into a jumping place. But wanton, unnecessary damage always causes irritation. Neil aims to build fences which are stock-proof but jumpable, a task he maintains is becoming increasingly difficult as big, Limousin cattle are better performers than a few of the horses.

Neil sees most of what goes on during the day, and forms his own judgments. He does not consider hunting cruel, for 'In my opinion I've never seen a frightened fox; he always believes he's going to get away.'

He was also there to help when a much respected Master lay still after a fall. Another helper begged 'Give him air – keep back' and a third suggested 'Loosen his clothes.' Neil proposed 'Give him a drop of whisky', at which the Master opened one eye, remarked 'Neil normally gets things right', and shut it again.

His ready wit rarely deserts him. He was recently invited with a group of Meynell farmers to spend a day at Highgrove as a guest of the Prince of Wales. When he was presented, the Prince remarked 'I didn't recognise you.'

'I didn't recognise myself when I looked in the mirror this morning,' replied Neil.

His charm is irresistible and must have saved the Meynell from many difficulties. 'There would not be half as much trouble if they'd promote you to a Joint Master,' someone told him recently. But to Neil that would not be promotion but demotion!

A MEMBER OF THE FIELD –
THE HOUSEWIFE

Mrs Amanda Agnew

Mandy Agnew lives in an attractive house within a stone's throw of Gatwick Airport. Her husband Ian has his own printing business some forty miles from home. His sporting interests include hill climbing in an historic Formula 3 car and some shooting. One son has just left the army after six and a half years and the other is in the film industry. Mandy herself is a superb cook and beautifully turned out. Unlike most of their neighbours', the garden does not include a tennis court or swimming pool. Instead, there are two loose boxes, a tack room, small hay barn and paddock.

Mandy first started hunting when she was nine, with the Surrey Union, where she still hunts. Her grandfather, with whom she lived for much of her childhood, had been Master of the Delhi Foxhounds and was a wonderful judge of a horse. He encouraged and taught her and soon she became interested in showing. Her two most successful show horses were the lightweight Grand Slam and the small hunter Clun Castle. As chairman of the British Bloodstock Agency, her grandfather came across a number of quality horses which had not quite made the grade in training.

Unfortunately the showing curtailed her hunting, for although she hunted the working hunters, she was frightened to bring the others out with hounds, because of the risk from other horses. Then after her marriage, when the children were small, she more or less gave up riding all together for ten long years, despite keeping her much loved brown mare for the whole of that time. She bred from the mare, and occasionally rode her, but mostly left her running out with her mother's cattle.

Then in 1974 a close friend said to her 'Come on, let's go hunting' and 'from that moment on I have not stopped.' The long break seemed to have given both her and the mare renewed enthusiasm: after six years the mare was showing no signs of old age when, at the age of 22, she tragically died of a twisted gut. Some five years before that, Mandy had been offered the pick of a yearling, mare or foal following the death of their owner. On the advice of a knowledgeable friend, she picked the foal, a chestnut filly, although it was not even weaned at that stage. She called it Demelza. Today Demelza is 14: she did 39 days hunting last season, and throughout her life she has been schooled, ridden and looked after almost entirely by Mandy. Despite initial problems with her jumping, overcome with the help of a few lessons for horse and rider, she is now a most reliable performer with beautiful manners.

Mandy works hard for her hunting for she has no help with Demelza and little in the house. Her husband is 'a wonderful support', not only at home but also to the hunt, helping and often doing the announcing at the point-to-point and similar functions. On her side, she does not allow hunting to interfere with aspects of their life which she considers important. Apart from feeding Demelza, she never starts work on her until her husband has set off for the office at 7.30, and for this reason she rarely does much cubhunting. Wednesday's dinner

Mrs Amanda Agnew. (*Trevor Meeks*)

is always put ready on Tuesday, and Saturday's on Friday, to allow for all contingencies on hunting days.

Living as she does on the edge of the Surrey Union country, many meets can be as much as an hour's drive away in the trailer. Mandy takes two hours to complete the chores before hunting, including plaiting, which only takes her ten minutes. She generally stays out with hounds until between three and four in the afternoon and likes to get everything straight that evening, so it is a long day. At least now that her sons are grown up, this is possible, where once her eye had always to be on the clock, in readiness for the school run.

She also plays an active part in the hunting community. She is an Area Manager for her part of the country, one of the most built up and difficult districts, with large numbers of very small landowners and tenants, but also a district which is only hunted two or three times a season. She prepares the packed lunches for fence judges at the hunter trials and is involved in catering for the point-to-point, farmers' dinner and other events. Recently she ran a most successful ferret racing evening, a fund raiser which was much enjoyed.

Unfortunately that evening also resulted in her name and telephone number being discovered by the anti-hunting brigade, who are so unpleasant and often violent in this part of Britain. A great animal lover – the family includes three dogs, an aviary, an aquarium, bantams and doves as well as Demelza – Mandy admits that out hunting 'I look the other way at the end, I'm afraid', despite having lost innumerable bantams, as well as a much loved pet lamb, to foxes.

Whilst in some parts of the country there are plenty of fences, albeit sometimes part of a cross country course, from other meets no-one will have the chance to leave the floor. Mandy enjoys both forms of hunting: 'I love the riding and I love watching hounds work.' She is only sad that local conditions make hunting so difficult, with long runs a rarity and the opportunities for watching hounds much restricted. She no longer enjoys competitive riding, and whilst 'On some days I feel like jumping absolutely anything, on other days I go round; I've got to the stage now where I don't have to prove anything to myself or anyone else. I refuse to terrify myself.' On the other hand, a number of nasty falls have certainly not put her off. 'If you've got a horse like Demelza who says 'Come on, let's get going', it makes you so confident even if you're having what I call a wobbly day. I love being out: I have a lot of friends hunting and we have a lot of laughs. I don't know what else I'd do if I didn't hunt.'

10

THE HORSE DEALER
Willie Darling

'It's not a great thing selling horses next door to where they've come from, because if they go better than they did for the first owner it doesn't please him and if they go worse it doesn't please the new one.' This was one of the reasons behind the enormous trade in horses, now slackening, between Britain and Ireland. Willie Darling has been dealing in horses for over fifty years from his farm near Durham in the Braes of Derwent country: he has also been a magistrate for over twenty years. Until recently, most of his horses were being imported from Ireland to sell in this country.

He worked successively with two close friends in Ireland, the second of whom, Tom Moore, was Master of the County Down Staghounds for thirteen seasons, but he himself went over frequently. He learnt to negotiate in that country, where tact is required to convince a proud owner that his horse is worth less than half the figure he imagines without causing lasting offence. Others never managed this: one dealer, whose blunt approach had shown many Yorkshiremen previously unsuspected faults in their horses, had to ask Willie Darling to do his buying in Ireland. Sometimes the owner would be prepared to return £100 or £200 on an £800 horse 'for luck', provided the full figure was on the cheque to show his friends.

Most of these horses had courage and would jump, but were very green. The system for breaking a young horse in Southern Ireland at the time was to back it in a lane between high, untrimmed hedges, then ride it until it was exhausted. Taking these out with hounds a few days after their arrival in England, as Willie Darling did, required remarkable skill and nerve. He preferred plough to grass on such occasions.

A group of farmers who went to Ireland to find themselves horses returned well pleased to await the arrival of their purchases. The first and most expensive came off the train for his new owner to ride him home, but bucked him off three times before they had left the station. The second, a grey, ran away with his owner. Both soon arrived in Mr Darling's yard, and both eventually made good horses. The grey, however, was almost sent back. Six months after he was sold, the owner rang up to say that in his yard horses were fed out of containers on the floor. This horse was causing concern as he could not eat without going down on his knees. The dealer replied that they must put him out in a field and if he could not eat grass standing up he would take him back.

Willie Darling on The Yank, Champion Hunter at Dublin Show 1970. (*Irish Times*)

Some horses inevitably come back because they do not suit their owners. Like most dealers, he does not allow horses to go out on trial, except perhaps with hounds for an hour, but will exchange an unsatisfactory horse for a different animal. Others he welcomed back when they had served their turn with a particular person. Many competent farmers would buy green horses from him, hunt them for a season and sell them back to be passed on as made hunters. The Simpson family in the Zetland country have bought one or two such horses from Willie Darling every year since the War.

At one time, Mr Darling would leave home at 7 p.m., drive his lorry to Heysham and sleep on the passenger boat reaching Ireland at 6.30 a.m. Here his Irish friends would meet him with their lorry and they would spend the day looking at horses, returning with those they had bought in time to load them at 6.30 p.m. He and his purchases could be home by lunch time. Changes in regulations, intended to benefit the horses, but which on the first occasion they were operative, in fact resulted in an additional 24 hours in transit for them, led him to abandon this system.

An annual highlight for many years was the Dublin Horse Show, where he showed horses bought by his friends with considerable success. In 1970 they won the Championship with The Yank. Showing in Ireland could be a nerve-wracking business, for these horses too were green. Once a renowned horseman from England was judging at Belfast for the first time when Willie Darling was drawn in first. As the judge approached to ride his horse, he warned him that it was green and not used to the double bridle, but the judge mounted carelessly and the horse came over backwards. Fortunately, neither was hurt, nor, re-markably, was the horse turned out of the ring. The second judge, more experienced in Irish ways, ignored his colleague's advice not to ride the horse, liked it and placed it first. It subsequently also won the Ladies' class. Other horses would find themselves working most of the night before the show when their owners had misgivings about the riding abilities of a particular judge.

A close friend and associate is Tony Dickinson, father of Michael, the eminent trainer, whose first pony Willie Darling supplied. Arthur Stephenson too has been a friend since teenage days. Mr Darling first took him to Ireland and introduced him to connections from whom he has been buying horses ever since. Willie Darling himself has found horses for most of the leading hunting families in the north of England and elsewhere. He particularly enjoyed hunting with the Zetland in the 1950s, when Lord Barnard and Captain MacAndrew were Masters. At that time there might be thirty or forty horses hunting on a Saturday that he had found, and he often took four out in his lorry in the morning and returned with only three. Occasionally his small son would have to be quietened, as when a loose horse galloped past and the boy squeaked 'Daddy, there's our chestnut horse!' But generally buyer and horse were well matched. It is always easier with a good rider: Douglas Nicholson, then chair-man of Vaux Breweries, was a superb horseman. He had some outstanding horses from Willie Darling, including Sea Knight who won the Foxhunter at Liverpool twice and was second at Cheltenham beaten a neck, and Merry Messenger, who was placed at Badminton. Colonel Cookson bought high class big blood horses for himself and his family from Willie Darling for more than thirty years. Less competent riders, including some who never left the floor, could also be found the right horse. At Dublin each year a previous owner asked after one outstanding hunter: successful though it was, it had never been asked to jump a fence since it reached its new home. Some buyers do not mind what a horse is like, provided the price is right.

If a novice approaches a dealer for a horse, 'You're foolish if you don't look after them a bit. One horse can do you a lot of harm, far more than ten good ones.' Most, wisely, bring an adviser with them; a few would be better without, where the 'adviser' rings beforehand to discuss how much there is for him. The merits of a horse are hard to evaluate: one Irishman wanted to know how a horse could be worth the price being asked for it. The seller assured him that it was half-brother to a famous racehorse. 'At home,' he replied, 'we are one mile from the station. I can run there in eight to ten minutes. My brother can't do it in less than half an hour, and he's my full brother!'

11

THE FELL HUNTSMAN
Barry Todhunter

As huntsman of the Blencathra, Barry Todhunter is following in a great tradition. His country is part of that hunted by the only huntsman whose name is known throughout the world, John Peel. His hounds are descended from John Peel's hounds, for on that great man's death several of his hounds were acquired by John Crozier, Master of a pack then popularly known as the 'Threlkeld Fox Dogs', but later called the Blencathra. He is successor, too, to an almost equally legendary figure in hunting circles, Johnny Richardson, to whom he whipped in from 1973 until Richardson's death in 1988.

Some aspects of fell hunting seem almost unchanged since the time of Peel. Many packs were once 'trencher fed', or kept, not in kennels, but in couples with farmers who would bring them to the meet each hunting day, then take them home at night. The Blencathra are kennelled during the hunting season but in theory during the summer hounds return to the farms where they were walked. The hunt staff are then laid off and expected to find their own employment.

In practice, a number of hounds are unable to go out to walk, perhaps because there is nowhere for them to go. Sometimes they will not stay at walk but set out on their own for the kennels whenever an opportunity arises. Others will return to the kennels for short periods, when their walkers are on holiday or ill, or a bitch is in season. The huntsman has to look after these hounds, bringing in flesh and skinning, attend hound shows and parade hounds at various local functions as a public relations exercise. He also takes most of the responsibility for visiting farmers, much of which has to be done in summer. In between all this he must find himself sufficient paid employment to maintain himself and his family, which he does by driving wagons, laying tarmac, fencing, cutting grass and similar work.

It is a job which requires dedication. Barry Todhunter was first taken hunting by his parents in a carrycot. As a boy, when hounds were near his Caldbeck home, he feigned 'flu except when an enlightened headmaster took the whole school to the meet in the morning then devoted the remainder of the day to writing and drawing about hunting. When he left school at fifteen, in 1970, the post of whipper-in to the Lunesdale was advertised. To his surprise and delight,

Barry Todhunter with the Blencathra Hounds and the legendary
Johnnie Richardson (*left*). (*Jim Meads*)

his application was successful, though from 'school to a fell pack was a fair step.
It was physically very hard, tiring and sometimes bewildering.' All the same,
two seasons later, he was loath to leave his many friends there when the
Blencathra were looking for a whipper-in, but could not miss the opportunity
to return to his home country and work under Johnny Richardson. 'He was a
very knowledgeable man in a lot of things, not just hounds and hunting. He was
a very popular man. He was liked by the farmers, and he liked and encouraged
children.'

Whilst so much remains unchanged, the Lake District itself has altered enormously even during Barry's own career. There is a divide between agriculture and tourism, and the sheer weight of people and traffic is a constant problem, the two main roads in Blencathra country a constant stream of cars nose to tail throughout the summer. Elsewhere, hunting not only suffers from the problems common to the whole district, but itself inadvertently adds to them: 'the little valley roads designed for a horse and cart weren't designed for 300 cars.' This is a constant anxiety and distraction to the huntsman, who is struggling to find ways in which to minimise disruption to the life of the local community. Only a small proportion of hunt followers walk with hounds, the majority staying in their cars, often wisely, for this gives them a much wider perspective of the sport than the fifty yards or so visible to a walker on the fellside.

Followers, particularly around Easter when other packs have finished hunting, come from all over Britain, and sometimes abroad. A cap is only taken on certain nominated days, and the season's subscription averages £5: this unrealistic approach, like so much else, is traditional. Yet there is tremendous support for the hounds locally, particularly amongst the farming community. New walks for hounds are always being added to the list, hunt functions as well as meets are well attended, and the annual Old Hound and Puppy Show, which also includes an open hound show, hound trails (for non-hunting, privately owned hounds) and sheepdog trials, is immensely popular.

The Blencathra are important for the farmers. As Barry says, 'I'm there to catch foxes, but nothing pleases me more than to show sport in the process.' This becomes particularly clear at the end of the season when the pack goes on to 'lambing call'. For the rest of the season hounds meet at 9.30 and finish around 2.30 p.m. In spring, no meets are fixed, but hounds are taken, sometimes as early as 4.30 a.m., to the lambing pens of any farmer who has had problems with foxes worrying his sheep. The object is to catch the particular culprit and return to kennels as soon as possible. A cast is made in the immediate area in the hope of picking up the drag of the fox, the scent he left going away from the pens, possibly several hours earlier.

The fell hound requires different characteristics from his cousin in the shires. Cry is important to enable them to work together: an old song refers to 'The deep mouthed pack of Blencathra.' They also need 'a different outlook on life. They've got to think for themselves', show common sense and initiative, and work together. If a fox goes up a crag, climbing through a gully near the top which is impenetrable to hounds, it is no good hounds remaining there marking. They must return to the bottom and divide, half working round each side, then joining up again when one strikes off the line where the fox emerged.

As well as the dangers common to all packs from traffic, fell hounds face other hazards from the nature of the country, such as being pushed off a narrow ledge above a precipice. The huntsman has always to be on his toes, under constant pressure as he strives for perfection. It is an immense relief to Barry when all his hounds are safely back in kennels after hunting.

No-one can be more conscious of the risks than he is, for in 1985 he had an accident which he was lucky to survive at all. It is a remarkable tribute to his determination and courage that he was able to take on the huntsman's job early in 1988, for he had spent some nine days in intensive care and eighteen months in and out of hospital. Terriers are normally strictly controlled, but on this occasion two managed to get to ground in a big, rocky place, still coupled to each other. Barry, as whipper-in, tried to untangle them. The huntsman was not with them at that moment, so a follower held hounds back on a rocky ledge above. A step forward resulted in the rock falling and crushing Barry. He was underneath it for two hours before he could eventually be winched to a helicopter.

Since then, he has made his own reputation for showing sport and killing foxes. So the legends surrounding the huntsmen of the Blencathra are constantly added to. Barry Todhunter is a worthy successor to John Peel.

THE TERRIER MAN AND
EARTH STOPPER

Roger Bigland

Roger Bigland is always downstairs drinking his tea by 4 a.m. On hunting days, which were five days a week when he was with the Heythrop, he likes to do as much earth-stopping for the day's draw as possible from around 5 a.m. onwards. At this time, the badger is generally back underground and will have no need to undo the earthstopper's work before the day's sport, whereas the fox is probably still out.

Following guidelines recommended by the Masters of Foxhounds Association and the National Trust, earths under his control are usually stopped with soil only, and do not require unstopping after hunting in the evening: neither fox nor badger will have any difficulty in doing this job for himself. The disturbance to badgers is halved if earths are only visited once. The badger population in the Cotswolds is enormous and continues to increase. Roger Bigland easily convinces those, usually newcomers to the country, who are concerned about the effect of his activities on badgers, that their fears are groundless. Such people 'seem to think they bring all the wildlife in the furniture van when they come.' They forget how badgers have thrived for generations in hunting country, for 'there's no doubt that foxhunters are the greatest conservationists of all,' keeping quiet places and hedgerows intact.

Roger Bigland himself, remarkably, did not come from a sporting or even countrified background. However, a family friend, Jack Fitchew, a keen and knowledgeable car follower with the Meynell and South Notts, took him to the Opening Meet of the Meynell in his MG sports car. Roger never forgot that day: 'I just absolutely got the bug from day one!'

Two ladies in a car also befriended him: they turned out to be Miss Elsie Wilson, Master of the Barlow, and her sister, the present Master, Miss Anne Wilson. When Roger left school at sixteen, they offered him a job in the Barlow kennels, but his parents were horrified. Accordingly, he went instead into the clothing industry. 'I hated every minute of it, though, funnily enough, I was quite successful at it, and lived for Saturdays.'

At 21 he advertised for a job as hunt terrierman, hoping to find a pack which hunted at least four days a week, so that he would not have to work also in kennels or fencing, and was delighted to be offered a job with the Cotswold. His wages dropped to £5 per week, plus £4 for his lodgings, but 'I thought I was the cat's whiskers!' Then he met Bill Peart.

There have always been two types of earth-stopper, one responsible for overseeing the whole country, and others in every district stopping the earths in their own particular patch. Roger Bigland soon found that doing a job part-time on an amateur basis was very different from full responsibility for four days' hunting a week. He was lucky, though, in being befriended by two remarkably knowledgeable countrymen. Bill Peart, who stopped the earths above Cheltenham racecourse, soon made the young man realise how little he knew, with his own encyclopaedic knowledge of the movements and whereabouts of every fox for miles around. Fascinated as he was by foxes and the life of the countryside, Roger eagerly absorbed all that he could learn. His second new friend, Bill Stainer, helped him to understand another, equally important, side of his work: he was head keeper on a large estate.

After seven seasons, Roger Bigland moved to the Heythrop country, where there are 85 shoots and nearly 50 professional keepers. In 1990 he moved again, to the North Cotswold, another big shooting country. He works throughout the summer at building up a good relationship with the keepers and helping with any problems which may arise. He is busy in summer too with the maintenance of coverts. To hold foxes, coverts have to be laid every few years, cut down to provide sufficient undergrowth for foxes to lie in. Tall trees with little beneath offer no security to foxes.

In winter, the country for each day's hunting has to be stopped so that foxes will not immediately run to ground. Roger Bigland will do the bulk of this himself, often accompanied by the key local man, keeper, farmer or farm man perhaps. The rest he will have to organise with the part-time earth-stoppers in the area. It is much harder today to find enough of these, with farms employing one man where once there were five.

During the day's cubhunting, Roger Bigland rarely uses his vehicle, but walks with hounds, accompanied by two of his terriers, and takes lifts with local helpers when necessary. His predecessors would have followed hounds on a cob, terriers with them in a bag. If hounds mark to ground, he is ready, though 'If you've done your job, you shouldn't be letting the terrier off the lead very often.' Whether a fox is then bolted, for hounds to hunt after being given a reasonable start, humanely destroyed or left alone, is not the haphazard decision it sometimes appears, but depends largely on the wishes of the Master, farmer, keeper or landowner.

Working terriers is a highly skilled business, made somewhat easier today by the use of electronic locators on the terriers' collars which indicate precisely where to dig. Thus less digging is necessary, saving both time and disturbance to the earths, and the risk to the terriers is reduced. In a lifetime, Roger Bigland has lost three terriers in just two separate accidents. He now seldom uses two together if he can avoid it, considering this increases the danger. He favours Jack

Roger Bigland with two of his terriers. (*Jim Meads*)

Russells, but also has Lakelands. Keeping some ten terriers, he is grateful for
family help with the kennel work at home.

In summer he is frequently asked to judge at terrier shows, and has even
travelled to Germany and the United States to do so. He much enjoys seeing the
different types of terrier popular in different regions, and regrets the modern
trend to standardisation.

Roger Bigland's job is not one which would appeal to many people, with low
pay and long hours. But for a man with his interest in the countryside, in foxes
and in terriers, it has given him all that the clothing industry could not offer.

13

THE HUNTING PARSON
The Reverend Rex Hancock

'A member of an endangered species' is how the Reverend Rex Hancock describes himself, and, with proposals for banning hunting on church land under discussion, sporting parsons seem unlikely to increase in numbers. Yet, more than a century ago, in 1882, an article bewailing their scarcity was published in *Baily's Magazine*, a year before the death of the most famous of them all, Jack Russell. Whilst most of the terriers which bear his name today bear little resemblance to those he owned, their fame is a fitting tribute to a remarkable man. Even at the age of 82, he would ride home 25 miles after a day's staghunting, and his funeral was attended by more than a thousand people.

Despite the fears expressed in the article, others have followed in Jack Russell's footsteps. Amongst the most famous were Cecil Legard and Jack Milne. Legard, rector of Cottesbrooke in Northamptonshire, edited the *Foxhound Kennel Stud Book* for nearly forty years, as well as judging both horses at Dublin and hounds at Peterborough, an unusual combination, before his death in 1918. Parson Milne was Master and huntsman of the Cattistock for the first thirty one seasons of this century.

Rex Hancock too is a West Country man. His grandfather and grandmother were both Masters of the Dulverton (East), which his father also hunted, and his father and mother were both Masters of the Devon and Somerset Staghounds. At Cambridge, Rex Hancock whipped in to the Trinity Foot Beagles in his first year, became Secretary in his second and hunted them in his final year, thus earning 'a first class degree in kennel management: I'm afraid academic work was rather pushed to one side.' In that season he had over eighty days' hunting in all, with beagles, foxhounds and staghounds. He particularly enjoyed taking the beagles to the north of England during the long vacation.

When he came down from Cambridge, he worked in the City, and it was then that he first felt the call to the ministry. After his ordination and two years as a curate, recollecting his enjoyment of National Service, he became an army chaplain.

He found this a most worthwhile calling, which also enabled him both to travel, and, in his free time in Britain, to hunt.

When stationed at Melton he hunted with the Cottesmore and the Belvoir, at

The Reverend Rex Hancock (*mounted*) taking an animal service.

Bovington with the South Dorset and Cattistock and at Catterick with the Zetland and Bedale, renewing his earlier enthusiasm for the north of England. Catterick was 'lovely if you liked field sports, but the bright lights merchants didn't like it so much.'

During the Falklands War, he volunteered to serve with the Task Force but was turned down because of his age, and shortly afterwards left the army and returned to the West Country, taking a group of seven parishes in the Quantocks. He now hunts very little, not through lack of inclination, but because his United Benefice and his chaplaincy with the Royal British Legion (Somerset and Avon) keep him fully stretched. This makes it all the more galling when the press portrays him as 'hunting five days a week to the neglect of my duties.' Such charges have always been levelled at hunting parsons, sometimes with cause, though the sport has often created a bond between parson and parishioners.

Mr Hancock still sees hunting as 'the golden thread that binds the countryside together' and feels that 'traditional sports have still a tremendous part to play.' He is very conscious of the effect the abolition of hunting would have on many of his parishioners, and the unemployment which would ensue. But he is also conscious that many of those now living in West country villages are 'not in actual fact country people'. They have spent their lives working in towns and cities, then retired to the country which they have known only on holidays. The risk is that they will then 'impose their rather suburban attitude on the genuine country people who have done so much for the countryside and (made it) such a marvellous place and so beautiful.'

Such an outlook, combined with a fear of extremists, was the root cause of a recent Parish Council request to Mr Hancock to cancel his annual Animal Service, a request which saddened him greatly. He usually conducts this mounted, with hymns played by the Watchet Town Band, of which he is President. Children bring all their different pets, and each receives a rosette. The cancellation particularly disappointed him because of plans to include a deputation from Riding for the Disabled. Mr Hancock supports this charity in other ways already, including playing the part, again mounted, of Mr Soapey Sponge in a pageant.

Mr Hancock does his best to ensure that the church and the countryside work in double harness, at least in his parishes. He is conscious, for instance, of how well churchyards lend themselves to conservation projects, being free of insecticides and pesticides, and offering scope for the planting of trees. He helped with a television documentary on this topic, but unfortunately a technical problem prevented the programme from being shown.

No man can hunt six days a week and satisfactorily combine this with a full time job away from the hunting field. Those few clerics in the past who attempted to do this inevitably neglected their parishes. But everyone needs relaxation, and country parishioners can only benefit from a parson whose interests, like theirs, lie in the countryside.

Ian Tweddall (*right*) and his father Stan Tweddall shoeing a horse. (*James Buxton*)

14

THE BLACKSMITH

Ian Tweddall

I an Tweddall is the fifth generation of his family to become a blacksmith. He works in partnership with his father Stan and his brother Bryan at Eppleby, not far from the Zetland kennels in North Yorkshire. They shoe most of the horses hunting with the Zetland as well as many of the Bedale and South Durham horses, and even extend as far as Cumbria. They are equally busy in summer, with eventers, racehorses, stud work, ponies and hacks. This is fortunate, for in some districts there can be considerable seasonal variation. Not only has their own family business expanded in the last ten years, with the three of them now working together, but, Ian says, 'the horse population in the area has snowballed, as people have more leisure time.'

Just after the War, Ian's father, then in partnership with his own brother, combined the blacksmith's business with running a pub. Much of their work at the forge was not with horses, but estate work on iron railings, repairs and so on. Many of the horses were heavy horses, used for business rather than leisure. Perhaps surprisingly, a higher proportion of the shoeing was done with the blacksmith travelling rather than the horse being brought to the forge, even though, in the days before portable gas forges, this meant that the horse had to be shod cold except in those yards where the owner had his own forge.

Blacksmiths today have often to work closely with vets to sort out foot problems in horses. 'I do quite a bit of surgical shoeing. Once you get a vet or two that recommend you . . . There are two or three good horse vets round here and I get on well with them.' Ian finds it easier today when he will usually talk to the vet himself on the telephone. Once, such communications were often made through the medium of owner or groom and this could lead to misunderstandings.

The relationship between vet and blacksmith is not always so harmonious. Friction may be caused over septic corns or gravel in the foot. Owners tend to approach their farrier first, but Ian points out that it is not for the blacksmith to treat lameness, although vets will often ask him to cut out the affected area and release the poison. Whilst some corns are caused by shoes digging in to the seat of the corn, horses with the bone roughened by pedal ostitis are more susceptible to them, just as thin soles will more easily be punctured by flints and shards, allowing dirt to get in. Some horses suffer terribly from pipe corns, where a channel develops allowing infection to enter. The great steeplechaser Crisp, whom Ian shod after his retirement from racing, suffered from this in his latter years. The release of the pus can cause owner as well as horse considerable relief: the acute pain and consequent filling of the leg may have led him to suspect tendon problems.

Whilst hunters used to do more road-work before and after hunting, hacking all over the country, they undoubtedly did considerably less during the day's sport. Steady road-work with a newly shod horse helps to get the shoes bedded in: they are less likely to be lost than if the horse is taken straight into deep going. Hammering on the roads behind hounds benefits no-one. It has increased the need for road studs or nails to prevent slipping. Ian does not favour studs in front, which can cause excessive wear to one part of the foot, though he sometimes uses nails. 'The front feet are supposed to slide; it reduces concussion. You want to keep the horse on his feet, but allow a certain natural slide.' Some types of shoe are more prone to slipping than others. Wider, flatter ones provide more protection for the foot, but concave shoes slip less. Horses come to rely on studs when they are used to them.

Owners and grooms can help their horses not only in the way they ride them ('Some people look after their horse and there's no problem, others treat them like motorbikes and get into trouble') but by telling the blacksmith how they are going. If he knows that a particular horse is given to overreaching, for example, he can fit a suitable shoe.

Ian sometimes works with the BHS Welfare officer on horses whose feet have been appallingly neglected. In the most extreme cases it is kinder to have them put down. But, he says, 'more ponies are hurt with kindness than cruelty', when overfeeding leads to laminitis. The new plastic shoes can help here, though Ian thinks that it will be a long time before they become a commercial proposition generally. Other complaints may benefit from the use of one of the foot cushions or pads on the market, though variations on these are sometimes produced with insufficient research, and almost all increase the likelihood of losing a shoe.

In emergencies, the family team cover for each other, even where usually 'some people prefer my brother, or me.' But Christmas is always difficult with 'over 200 horses out on Boxing Day, including some people who haven't hunted from one year to the next.'

Ian was trained by his father and then trained his brother. The firm has recently taken on its first outside apprentice as Stan Tweddall wishes to do less. As apprentices can now be taken on only by farriers on an approved training list, Ian receives some five or six requests a month. The apprenticeship lasts four years and a quarter of that time has to be spent at college, much more than when Ian trained. He feels that the theoretical education is excellent, even if the requirement for English and Maths O-level would have mystified some of the great, but illiterate, blacksmiths of the past. But it can be difficult for the employer to spare the apprentice for so long, and only practical experience can reveal which trainees have that prime requirement, 'a bit of a gift in handling horses.'

When Ian encounters a difficult horse, he tries first to find why it is troublesome: some are frightened of the noise, some have been mistreated, some have back problems or arthritis. Here lifting the leg differently can help. If he has not shod the horse before, but it comes from the same district, he may recognise the work of a particular farrier, and telephone him to ask for guidance. He carries the shoe sizes of most of the horses he shoes in his head, and makes some thirty per cent of his own shoes.

He enjoys taking part in competitions, but finds it time-consuming. 'I'm quite happy if I get a place. A lot of the lads do the circuit. They get to know what (particular) judges are looking for.' He favours prizes at local shows for the best shod horse in the show: 'it gives you a bit of incentive.'

In the course of his work, Ian Tweddall has met a wide range of people, amongst them distinguished visitors to the area needing help in an emergency, from members of the royal family to Red Rum. The Tweddall family has a business which is demanding, but interesting and varied. Their customers benefit from their skill and dedication, and the accumulated experience of five generations.

15

A MEMBER OF THE FIELD –
THE BUSINESSMAN
David Parkes

D avid Parkes did not hunt until he was twenty-one, when he was doing his National Service on public duties in London. His first day was a Monday with the Quorn. It was made the more terrifying by the presence in the field of almost all his senior officers. After hunting, he received 40 extra pickets, for being improperly dressed (wearing brown garter straps with white breeches), with the proviso that he should hunt on all 40 of these days.

Apart from riding as a child and some regimental polo, he had little experience of horses. He had always been interested in dogs and hounds; indeed his first business included the ownership of 550 greyhounds, cared for by 55 kennelmaids. Partnering his brother in this enterprise benefitted them both: his brother had his own cricket team so David worked long hours particularly over weekends in summer. In winter the position was reversed, as he had taken up hunting.

Six months after leaving the army he got married. His father-in-law had been secretary of the Waterford Hounds between the wars. Soon the new convert to the sport was living in Kensington and flying to Ireland as Master and Field Master of the Waterford on Saturdays and Tuesdays, with Sundays with the Kilmoganny Harriers and Mondays with either the Kilkenny or the Tipperary. Perhaps as a result of this experience he now considers it imperative that Masters and Field Masters should be easily available, ideally living in the country.

His first marriage did not last, and when he left Ireland he also gave up hunting. Some fifteen years later, when he was remarried and living in Hampshire, his son Harry was encouraged to hunt by his preparatory school. Antoinette, Harry's mother, who had hunted once in her childhood, decided to accompany him, and soon all three were hunting with the Hampshire Hunt. Whilst their son's involvement was short-lived, both his parents moved to the Wilton after a season and then, after trying a horse with the Cattistock, started hunting in that country regularly.

Today, David Parkes works part-time for a property company in central London. He and his wife live near Romsey in Hampshire, keeping the horses at home and hunting two, or occasionally three, days a week. They subscribe to both the Cattistock and the Blackmore Vale; whilst their Saturdays are almost always with the Cattistock, during the week they are thus able to pick whichever day or days is most convenient for his work. They usually also have a few days with the Heythrop each season: London's accessibility to different hunting countries has been appreciated ever since Mr Jorrocks described its railway stations as 'the best cover-hacks in the world.'.

The hunting businessman has two options for his horses. They can either be kept at livery in the country where they hunt, or, provided that the owner's wife is willing and able to take charge of the yard, they can live at home. The Parkes family prefer the latter solution, feeling that the detriment to the horses of long hours out of the stable is more than compensated for by the additional standard of care which is possible at home. This system also allows greater flexibility in choosing where and when to hunt. The horses leave the yard at 8 a.m. and are seldom home before 7 p.m. Mr Parkes usually has a second horse whilst his wife prefers to hunt a shorter day. They themselves travel by car, where a telephone enables him to make full use of the time.

They have six horses, and employ a head girl and two YTS girls, who only work a four day week each. Occasionally the head girl hunts for part of the day. She also often helps other people with problems, moving lame horses, or taking

David Parkes.

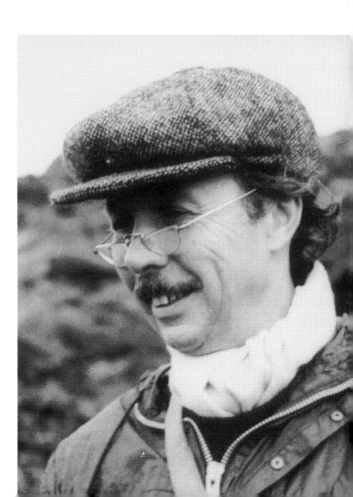

a horse home where its rider has had a fall. The season is a long one, for, after the Cattistock and Blackmore Vale finish, they hunt on Exmoor, still travelling from home, until 1st May.

Whilst much time would be saved and organisation simplified if he lived in Dorset, David Parkes is also very conscious of his responsibilities as a visitor in the Cattistock country. In common with other packs, the subscription is higher for those not resident. With the problems facing farmers today, he feels that the differentiation should be greater still, or perhaps take the form of a large initial joining fee. He considers that the cost of hunting is remarkably low compared with that of other field sports, 'say pheasant shooting where costs are two to three times higher. This increased rate should be imposed only on those like myself who wish to be visitor subscribers and hence entitled to hunt with their pack at will.' Realistically they are better able to support the hunt with their money than their time. This additional income should enable hunts to raise their standards of organisation, perhaps with more paid help, and to build up financial reserves for the future.

There are many ways in which guests can and should show their appreciation to their host country, through sponsorship of events, for example, or enabling the hunt, through interest-free loans or outright gifts, to buy an important covert. Their professional knowledge and business acumen can often also be turned to good account. Successful businessmen 'are used to identifying problems and causing them to be solved, and not moaning and groaning but doing nothing about it.' Their quest for a high standard of sport can have a stimulating effect on the countries they visit. The distance can also be 'a distinct advantage, for one is not involved in the minor politics and squabbling which exists in any hunting country', so that the outsider can sometimes act as intermediary.

Whilst he himself does hunt on Saturdays, others in a similar position will frequently hunt midweek only, and have other commitments at home at weekends. This helps to spread the load of large fields, which is so often a major problem for Masters and farmers on Saturdays. He does not hunt for the social scene, but likes to entertain some of his hunting friends in Hampshire in the summer, when he rarely visits Dorset, except perhaps for the Puppy Show.

David Parkes considers hounds 'the essence of it' and enjoys a day in a poorer part of the country with a much smaller field. All the same, 'hunting is a "Dare I?" activity; the excitement and fear results in one totally forgetting business and family affairs.' Hunting is 'a genuine sport: pheasant shooting is a pastime or recreation.' He defines sport as something which 'if done flat out involves the risk of serious injury or death' and sees this element as an essential part.

Modern transport has made the businessman hunting far from home a better known figure in the hunting field than he was in the past. If he is as aware as David Parkes is of his responsibilities as well as of his own interests, he will be sure of a welcome.

Mr Parkes became Master of the Wilton Hounds in 1991.

16

THE KENNELMAN
Ralph Stubbings

'I've always been interested in hounds or dogs, like, as other people are interested in horses.' This is how Ralph Stubbings, kennelman of the Heythrop, describes his choice of career. An impressive collection of trophies won by his greyhounds testify to his skill as well as his enthusiasm: for although the greyhounds have to be trained by a licensed trainer, 'I've always had them from a puppy, and I've raised them myself. You see them grow – it's a real pleasure to watch them.'

This affinity with dogs and hounds led to him following in the footsteps, not of his father, a renowned expert in the world of 'hedge plashing and tree felling', but of his father-in-law, who had been in hunt service as a kennelman all his life. Ralph, after three or four years in the army, started by serving his apprenticeship in the butchering trade. Then his father-in-law helped him to get the job of second kennelman at the Belvoir. 'It was real hard in them days. Everything was done by hand: very big yards to keep tidy. You had a lot more to do.'

He then moved on to the Garth as first kennelman during the great Mastership of Miss Effie Barker. He recalls hounds singing in kennels. 'They were beautiful singers. In the War, they used to try and keep in with the last little bit of the sirens.' Those moving soon afterwards into the new houses around the kennels would listen mystified, thinking there was a ghost about.

His next move was to the very different country of the Albrighton. 'You've got to have at least three or four moves to get the experience from one place to another, and then, yourself, you put it together: "I think that way's better."' Since then, he has also been at the Suffolk, Atherstone and Beaufort kennels. Badminton was an interesting place to work: not only did he get on extremely well with Brian Gupwell, the huntsman, but there was rarely a dull moment. One day an elderly member of his family glanced out of the window at a passer-by and remarked: 'See that woman? I've seen her before and I can't work out where I've seen her!' It was the Queen Mother.

Vital though his part is in the team, 'people don't realise, especially followers, what work a kennelman has to do.' His day starts early, particularly during cubhunting. As soon as hounds have left the kennels, he has to 'see to the yards, put down a nice clean bed and get the flesh ready for them when they come back from cubbing. Then there are one or two lame ones left behind what wants

Ralph Stubbings at the Kennels at Badminton when he was kennelman to the Beaufort. (*Jim Meads*)

seeing to. If there's any skinning you get that done, then get the list of people who rang up to fetch (flesh) in again.'

Collecting flesh from farmers has always been time-consuming. Traditionally, this is a service which hunts have offered to their farmers, who without it would have to bury or otherwise dispose of stock which dies. With farms spread over a wide area and flesh needing collecting with the minimum possible delay, it has probably never been the most economical way of feeding hounds. Difficulties have recently been aggravated since the companies who remove the offal, or unusable parts, now make a charge. Consequently, many hunts have now to pass on a proportion of the expense to the farmers, and a few are unable to offer the service at all. Ralph still travels the Heythrop country, bringing in flesh, and putting down animals where necessary.

This can be sad work for the kennelman, especially where horses are concerned. But Ralph ensures that it entails no suffering, mental or physical: rather it can be an end to pain. 'If they've had a good innings and it comes to an illness and they can't cure them, I think that's the best way out.'

Animals, like humans, are saved much pain by modern drugs. These also save time: when Ralph started work, a hound with a poisoned foot probably needed bathing several times a day for some days: today a single shot of penicillin will have the same effect. Ralph was glad too to see the barbarous custom of rounding hounds' ears ended soon after he entered hunt service.

He particularly enjoys his work with brood bitches and puppies. He takes trouble to befriend those bitches which are due to whelp, and is interested in the development of the puppies at every stage. Even the butchering side of his work interests him, for, as a vet once said to him when bringing some students to the kennels, 'they would learn more in six months here than they would in six years of paperwork.'

During his lifetime, Ralph has seen the work of the kennelman become easier with the development of labour-saving equipment. 'It's a healthy life, but you've got to be really interested to do it. You can earn a lot more doing something else and the hours are longer here. I know it's not a clean job or anything like that, but you do learn.' He has passed on this philosophy to his family: his son is now kennel huntsman of the Wheatland.

17

THE LIVERY YARD KEEPER

Anthony Steward

In a quiet lane, on the Fernie Opening Meet day, three yellow horse boxes draw up containing perhaps eighteen horses. Some ten people emerge from hastily parked cars, pulling on boots, fastening spurs, carrying hunting whips and gloves.

'Anthony, how's my other horse? Will he be right for Wednesday?'

'The traffic on the motorway this morning . . .'

'I've got my Quorn day on Monday. Where . . .?'

'I won't be able to hunt for ten days . . .'

'I've left my red coat behind, Anthony. What on earth can I do?'

Anthony Steward notes plans, reassures, and even supplies the forgetful one with his own black coat, finding a tweed jacket for himself. Another season has begun.

Anthony took over his big hunter livery yard from his father Jim Steward, whose clients included Lady Delamere, of *White Mischief* fame. Jim, like Anthony, combined it with farming and horse dealing.

Although livery yards have always existed, they have only come into their own since the last war. Nimrod described a young sportsman, up at Oxford around 1790, employing an experienced groom for his hunters, whilst his unsporting brother merely sent his hacks to a livery yard. A century later, the Duke of Beaufort reminded his readers that doubtless livery yards existed where horses would be 'as well cared for as they would be in their own stable at home. But such perfect places are not likely to be common . . .'

Even between the Wars, those unable to keep a horse at home were more likely to hire, possibly taking the same horse on a regular basis, than to keep one at livery. Today, with reliable staff hard to find and fewer homes having stabling, livery yards, both on a do-it-yourself basis and those like Anthony's which offer a full service, proliferate. 'Do-it-yourself' yards are excellent for those without stables. Others lack the time, or knowledge, to do their own horses, or live far from the country where they wish to hunt. For them, full livery is essential.

In a yard like Anthony's, the horses come in from grass, perhaps on his farm, early in September to start getting fit. Some will be cubhunting regularly. Others may not see their owners before the Opening Meet.

Anthony Steward out with the Fernie. (*Jim Meads*)

Most of Anthony's clients hunt with the Fernie, as he does himself, but his yard at Brigstock is ten miles from the nearest Fernie meet. This complicates the administrative side: an early start is necessary, horses are plaited the night before and there can be no slipping back for anything left behind. Everyone planning to hunt telephones on the preceding night to confirm plans.

Up to three lorries, driven by himself, his wife Jane and a third driver, depending on the number out on a particular day, take the horses, including any second horses, to an agreed point. As each person decides to go home, he or she removes the tack, puts a rug on the horse and leaves it tied up in the lorry. As each lorry is filled it is driven home.

Whilst several of Anthony's clients live in the country, some are professional men driving up from London for each day's sport, who depend on him for all their equestrian needs. Some have hunted all their lives, but others have come fresh to the sport. Anthony helps them to start hunting, finding, and where necessary schooling, the right horses for them.

At home, Anthony manages the farm and his other business interests. In summer he is often away at shows and has judged hunters or cobs at all the leading shows. He no longer takes part in show jumping or point-to-pointing, as he used to do. In winter the day-to-day running of the yard and care of the thirty or so horses, two-thirds liveries, the rest their own, are supervised by Jane, though Anthony's experience is often in demand when difficulties arise.

In the hunting field, Anthony is always busy. Whilst his own horse may be out to be schooled, tried or sold, he will find time to help anyone, client or otherwise, who needs him. Whether catching a loose horse, shutting a gate, having a word with a farmer or extricating a horse which has fallen into a ditch or tiger trap, he is there when needed. His ready smile, gentle charm and competent ability resolve endless problems. His tactful intervention has prevented many disagreements. A quiet word of advice on the right way to reach hounds has prevented many a thoughtless late arrival from unwittingly heading the hunted fox, or needlessly upsetting a farmer.

As a dealer, Anthony's exceptional eye for a horse combined with his experience both as a horseman and on the veterinary side stand him in good stead. Equally important, his understanding of people helps him to match the right horse to the rider. He keeps his own counsel: when asked out hunting what he was riding, his reply 'a chestnut horse' was given with such charm that it was some time before the questioner realised how little she had learnt.

Reuniting clients with their horses can prove interesting. One horse had succeeded in shedding not only its rider but bridle, martingale and saddle as well. Another client some years ago found the search for his missing steed expensive as he filled up a farmer's car with petrol to scour the countryside and offered drinks all round for information.

At last two small boys reported that their dad had shut a horse in his milking shed. It was now dark but Anthony found horse and saddle unscathed, and was about to go back to find the bridle. But the client had had enough. 'Forget it,' he said, 'and buy another.'

Few clients today can afford such an outlook. For most, their livery bills are buying not only the horse's keep but their own freedom from many of the worries of ownership. Anthony himself says 'In a business like mine you'll never get rich. But you'll have a lot of fun.'

18

THE VETERINARY SURGEON
Dr Richard Medd

Most people with demanding jobs find one of the attractions of hunting is that it allows them temporarily to forget everything else. For Dr Richard Medd this is impossible. He runs a veterinary practice single-handed and must always be available to his patients. He whips in to the Cambridgeshire Harriers with a radiopager in his pocket, ready, in case of emergency, to 'chuck my horse to Carol [his wife] and grab a lift. Fortunately it doesn't happen very often.'

Richard Medd hunted when possible with the Enfield Chace from the age of twelve, though he did not have his own horse until he was twenty-one. He also helped with the breaking of horses to harness, driving them, incredibly, on the North Circular. Originally a classicist at school, his decision to qualify as a vet necessitated a change to the science subjects. Gifted musically as well, sitting for an organ scholarship resulted in the offer of a place at Cambridge. He first started hunting with the Harriers during the mid fifties, when he was up at Cambridge, where he also played some polo. On his return to the area in 1969, after a period when he was unable to hunt, he started whipping in. He was then working full time in medical research at Huntingdon, and even now he continues to work in toxicology and surgical research.

Dr Medd was often asked by friends to treat their horses. The circle of 'friends' became impossibly wide, and in 1981 he established his practice, taking on every form of veterinary work, both routine and specialist. His research work is sometimes utilised here too: he carries out thoracic surgery on his own animal patients where necessary, and is able to offer them the standard of post operative care which is perhaps the most vital aspect of all in such cases. Whilst horses at first formed eighty per cent of his patients, the increase in small animal work means they now constitute only fifty per cent. His practice covers a huge area, between Corby, Diss and Grantham, and he is sometimes asked to travel further still to examine a horse for purchase.

To enable him to fit in all his commitments and to whip in to the Cambridgeshire Harriers two days a week, Dr Medd regards Sunday as an ordinary working day. His wife does their three horses, provides a marvellous back-up service in the surgery and on the hunting field and is always ready to take over in any emergency. During the hunting season, accidents are usually the only unpredictable calls, for there is little horse breeding in his area until later in the spring.

For Dr Medd, hunting is not a relaxation but a fresh challenge. 'The old type of amateur whip is out. On the hunting day you are not really an amateur; if you are you are really not much use.' Even so, he is always ready to help anyone having an accident during the day. He takes with him 'no more than any sensible

Dr Richard Medd and (*left*) kennel huntsman Philip Harris with the Cambridgeshire Harriers. (*Jim Meads*)

person ought to carry in a pocket, basically a controlling bandage, a good pad of gamgee and a pair of blunt scissors. If that is not enough, you need the whole carful.' If the hunting doctor is not out, he sometimes helps with human as well as equine casualties. Today, the first priority is often to move a horse to the right place for treatment, whereas in the past it would have been stabled at the nearest farm. 'People's expectations of what you can do increase. Even with fractures these days you aren't looking to put them down straight away. The problem is the soft tissue damage. If you can immobilise, transport and assess without soft tissue damage, then a fracture can often be repairable.' The vital factor is the speed with which the horse is pulled up in the first place.

In avoiding accidents, 'the first thing is basic fitness.' Tired horses are the most susceptible to injury. 'Just think also where you're putting your horse.' An unexpected soft patch in otherwise good going can be devastating, and, on setaside land particularly, deterioration in the drainage system leads to dangers.

Dr Medd sees no discrepancy between devoting most of his life to animal welfare and his love of hunting, for the hunted animal is 'either fit and very much alive or dead.' Indeed, hounds can provide a mercifully quick end for sick or wounded animals. Hunting also offers the chance for closer observation of what goes on in the countryside. He cites the big variation in the hare population, even within a single season and in a particular area, which is inherently mobile and has been recorded for many years. Today the finding of dead hares is often attributed to the use of gramoxone and other agrochemicals, but probably it is a virus problem.

Richard Medd puts an enormous amount into his sport off the hunting field as well as on it. He and his wife play a large part in the administration of the point-to-point, for example. His professional knowledge is invaluable. He has always treated hounds for the cost of drugs, but his expertise is increasingly in demand for help with such new issues as the EEC regulations affecting flesh collection. This is a problem confronting many hunts, who have traditionally combined the feeding of hounds with the provision of a much appreciated service to farmers. New legislation is making this system no longer economically viable.

Many vets qualifying today will go into industry, public health or other positions, rather than private practice, and a high proportion of the women qualifying 'will only be available probably for half of their working lives.' Indeed, Dr Medd regards the training, despite the extremely high academic standard required and the time involved, as 'a very good basic education leading into a lot of more specialist disciplines.' The hunting world is particularly dependent on those vets who are prepared to accept the disruptive nature of life in private practice. Few even of these are likely to contribute more to the sport than does Richard Medd. His combination of skill, expertise, energy and commitment is rare anywhere, and invaluable to hunting.

19

A MEMBER OF THE FIELD –
THE SCHOOLBOY
Luke Tomlinson

'At first I didn't really jump that much, then it clicked. I used to like my parents giving me a lead and telling me what it was like the other side. I like going my own way best now.' At the age of thirteen, Luke Tomlinson has had some five seasons of regular hunting with the Beaufort, and had occasional days even before that. His parents, Simon and Claire Tomlinson, have a large yard in Gloucestershire where polo is the first priority, but all the family hunt.

Luke started hunting on a leading rein, but his first pony was not the ideal confidence giver. 'It jumped, but it pulled me a lot and carted me round the place.' Then he was offered the loan of Biscuit, a thirteen hand pony which had been outgrown by his owners. 'He was really easy and quite old,' and he built up Luke's confidence and enabled him not only to enjoy riding across the Beaufort country, but also to watch hounds. 'I like the way hounds work, and they do most of the work,' he says.

He is sufficiently interested to spend a few days during his holidays at the kennels. He goes on his own, and 'I help a bit and I see what's going on and I learn. I wanted to find out what it was like.' He has also given considerable thought to the ethics of hunting. 'I like reading books about the fox, from both sides.' Several of his school friends do not approve of hunting, and he listens to their point of view, then in the car with his family he will put these arguments forward and listen to the answers his parents give. He finds that these discussions explain a lot about hunting.

Luke has been a weekly boarder at his school, coming home every weekend. 'But now I'll be going to a bigger school where I won't be allowed to come out, but they do have beagling there...' As a weekly boarder, he had half a day's hunting a week, leaving school at midday on Saturday and being taken to find his pony at the point agreed for the Beaufort second horses. Biscuit was succeeded by the younger, though smaller at 12 hands 2 inches, Tom Thumb, whom he is riding in the photograph, taken when he was ten or eleven. Tom Thumb has been a real family pony: Luke's older sister Emma had him 'when she was two and he was two', and now he has been taken over by Luke's younger brother Mark. Luke now has 'Jemima, who is just under 14.2, and she's very nice: not easy but not hard.'

Jemima is trace clipped and lives out. During the term time she is exercised for him, then groomed for hunting. 'After hunting I do my own pony and clean my own tack: that's the labour of it all!' He usually also rides on Sundays, and during the holidays does most of the work himself. In the summer, when the polo season is in full swing, he and Emma and Mark have a separate place to keep their tack away from the rest of the large yard, 'and we have to clean that and keep it in order. Sometimes we get a bit of help luckily.'

During the Christmas holidays, Luke likes to have as much hunting as possible, and sometimes he is fortunate enough to be lent one of his mother's

Luke Tomlinson on Tom Thumb hunting with the Beaufort. (*Stuart Newsham*)

horses, either to give Jemima a day off, or as a second horse, to give her a shorter day. His father is one of the Field Masters of the Beaufort, and Luke particularly enjoys the days when his father is in charge. 'It's more fun. He sends me on point and things like that.' He takes such responsibilities seriously, but is no longer worried that he will fail to see the fox. 'It's all about where you're placed. If there's a dip running along the field and you can't quite see then you're in trouble.'

Luke finds the Beaufort field kind and helpful. 'If there's a queue at a gate, they let me go. It's only the ones out of control really who cut across (at fences). They're very good, but some of them are a bit out of control, which puts the children off.' When he first started hunting, he was sometimes puzzled about what was happening, and was grateful for explanations, but 'I picked it up quite quickly as I began to like it more.' He was once kicked, 'by a big horse, and that put me off a lot. I tried to go past him in a narrow lane so it was my fault.'

Luke thinks that 'a lot of children go out just for social reasons. It's nice to see your friends out. They don't like the hound side so much.' One chance to watch hounds is largely denied him. He would like to do more cubhunting, but, with school terms starting earlier than in the past, this is rarely possible.

He enjoys the Children's Meets because of the chance they sometimes give him to go with the huntsman or the whipper-in for part of the day. He was given a hunting horn for Christmas, and has been busy practising: 'I'd like to hunt hounds one day.'

20

THE SCHOOL KENNEL HUNTSMAN

Nat Thornton

Boys who are lucky enough to go to one of the public schools with a pack of beagles have a marvellous opportunity to learn about hunting. Many of the outstanding Masters of Hounds today first learnt their job with a school, college or university pack. The guidance they receive at this stage is of lasting importance and usually depends almost entirely on one man, the kennel huntsman.

Nat Thornton has been interested in field sports all his life. Whilst he has never ridden to hounds, he has always hunted on foot, as a boy mostly with the Pytchley, and also enjoyed both shooting and fishing. Originally an engineer, he spent fourteen years working for English Electric. In his spare time he was hunting regularly with the Stowe Beagles. The old kennel huntsman was moving and one day Nat said to him:

'They tell me you're leaving at the end of the season – who's having your job?'

'You are,' came the reply.

Within a week he had been to Stowe for an interview and a month later the job was his. It is a most demanding position, for, with the exception of the schoolmaster who liaises between beagles and school authorities, he is the only official who is more than eighteen years old or who lives on the spot. Thus he is tied seven days a week and is unlikely to be able to have more than a week away from home each year.

The Stowe Beagles have been outstandingly successful on the flags in recent years. Gravity, Grasper, Sally and Redcap, and before them Starlight and Willow, have all excelled at Ardingly and Peterborough. Nat does all the breeding himself, having been helped in his first two or three seasons by his predecessor. In this as in everything else he always involves the boys, asking their opinions and trying to pass on to them his own exceptional eye for conformation. Showing decisions too are always made collectively, with the boys putting forward suggestions and Nat pointing out any glaring faults. A good hound who shows easily may be shown by two boys unaided, though when there is something important like a Championship Nat will probably take over.

Nat Thornton receiving a Championship Cup for the Stowe Beagles from HRH Prince Michael of Kent at the South of England Hound Show. (*Jim Meads*)

In kennels too the boys play a full part. Some of them in turns go down for an hour every day to feed hounds, walk them out in the magnificent grounds and clean out the kennels. When alterations to the buildings are needed, once again Nat takes charge with a labour force consisting solely of boys. One parent was heard to murmur that the only thing her son had learnt whilst away at school was how to lay bricks.

Most of the boys who are interested have a chance to whip in. When a new Master is ready to try his hand at hunting hounds, Nat gives him first some homework to study: old articles from *Horse and Hound*, some by Captain Wallace, others adapted from Ikey Bell by Daphne Moore, with the important points marked. On the way to the meet, they discuss how to handle that particular day's draw.

Nat emphasises that beagling is a circular motion and it is important to keep coming back into the draw. Afterwards they talk about how the day has gone, the successful parts and the aspects which could have been improved. One boy had problems with the horn, so Nat arranged for him to use one with a reed in. Nat will always help too with telephoning farmers and landowners to make the necessary arrangements, when the restrictions of school life make this difficult for the Master.

The collecting of flesh is usually left to Nat, although many farmers are very helpful. Boys occasionally help with skinning, though this is inevitably a slow business, for Nat recalls how he used to take an hour and a half for a sheep himself, whereas now he can complete the job in around six minutes. One benefit of the school environment is that a considerable amount of kitchen waste is available for hounds.

Under Nat's auspices, the beagles have become involved in charitable work, particularly through a local annual 'Honda and Hound' event, which in six years has raised £140,000 for charity. Hounds also parade at shows in the area, taken by the boys.

Local support outside the school is strong. Fields can number forty or fifty on a Saturday, excluding boys, and there is an excellent Supporters' Club, which, whilst the school pays the basic running costs, is often able to provide a few luxuries. Indeed, so popular is the pack in the district that Nat always warns Masters that, whilst an occasional Saturday visiting a different country may be of value, two in succession are not acceptable, even in school holidays.

Hounds themselves adapt remarkably well to a succession of different huntsmen and the turnover in Masters is inevitably fast. Most of the boys interested come from hunting backgrounds, though a few city boys have been able to discover a completely new way of life, occasionally even becoming Masters. Behind it all, stable and reliable, providing sport and education in equal measures, is the kennel huntsman. Nat Thornton and his colleagues in similar positions make a great contribution to the future of hunting.

Ephie Robson on Bone Idle. (*Jim Meads*)

21

THE FARMER
Ephie Robson

Ephie Robson farms 800 acres on the borders of the Morpeth and Tyne-dale hunting countries in Northumberland. A mixed farm, it includes arable, sheep and cattle. Stretches of rocks and heather are interspersed with first-class farming land. Hound puppies at walk explore the yard, young horses, a brood mare and hunters graze the paddocks. Mr Robson is also a National Hunt permit holder, training his own horses to run under rules as well as in point-to-points.

'Horses have had an enormous impact on our life, and the people that I've met. I can well imagine I'd be a very uninteresting, hard working farmer, probably much better off, had I not had an equine interest' is his own comment, though the 'uninteresting' part is hard to believe. The two sides of his life, work and sport, farming and horses, have neatly dovetailed together, with his wife sharing his enthusiasms. Young horses, many of them home-bred, are broken in by the girl groom, who never backs them until she has worn out a pair of boots long reining. She is also an excellent stockman, and here ridden horses too can play their part in the farm, moving cattle and sheep. The young horses are then schooled on by their owner, hunted and run in a few point-to-points and under rules before being sold. One home-bred horse won seven races for Mr Robson, another, bought in a batch of seven horses, won fifteen including seven three-mile chases. Bone Idle, since his sale, has gone on to become one of the top point-to-pointers in the south of England. The telephone rings frequently on Saturday evenings with news of other successes.

Mr and Mrs Robson have both hunted all their lives, and love having hounds over their land, well aware that with their light land, even if it looks appallingly badly cut up the following morning, there will be little or nothing to be seen a week later.

But they have every sympathy with non-hunting farmers, knowing how much trouble a crucial gate left open can cause.

Since winter corn became a viable prospect in the area, harvesting has often been completed by the end of September, enabling hunting to start earlier, but at the other end of the season 'There's nothing worse than upsetting a farmer by hunting too late and going through his ewes; it is a traumatic time enough without running into problems there.'

These and all the other difficulties which can arise are solved more easily in countries where Masters and Secretary have a rural background and understand the farming community's problems. Where this is not the case, Mr Robson feels that someone from the farming community might help with liaison, for so much is a question of diplomacy.

Similarly, a large number of hunting farmers and farmers' sons helps to improve relations with the rest of the farming community. The owner likes to see a few familiar faces amongst the crowd riding through his yard, some of whom will stop for a friendly word, responding with sympathy or even with wisecracks to his complaints. If too many of the field are strangers, unable or unwilling to communicate with the man whose land they are riding across, he will naturally be alienated. When such people ignorantly ride over wheat, leave gates open, break down fences or gallop unnecessarily down a wet grass slope, it is not surprising if he threatens to ban hounds from his land.

Some farmers, inevitably, are waiting only for an excuse to object to hounds. Even they, however, will often appreciate an invitation to some hunt function, a dinner, perhaps, a Fur and Feather lunch or a pass for the point-to-point. All are grateful for the service offered by the hunt in collecting deadstock, if this is done promptly and efficiently. It also provides an excellent opportunity for a tactful whipper-in or kennelman to learn of problems before they arise. Many non-hunting farmers, far from causing trouble, not only welcome hounds on to their land but will help in other ways, perhaps walking hound puppies or taking part in the ewe rearing schemes popular in this area. With these, the hunt will pay for a young ewe to be kept by the farmer who, whilst keeping the wool for himself, will return the value of all lambs she produces to the hunt.

Ephie Robson believes that the key to the future of hunting lies in the Pony Club. Here the farmers' sons and, perhaps predominantly, daughters, learn about hunting, the town children learn about the country and all come to know each other. As a boy, he was himself given much encouragement by the Master, being sent on to the end of the covert, sometimes whipping in and generally learning to appreciate hunting. If as many as possible of the farmers and farmers' wives of the future can enjoy similar opportunities, this will do much to bridge the gap between the farming and the hunting communities.

22

THE HUNTING ARTIST
Robin Furness

'Weather and landscape are the important things' for Robin Furness. All his hunting pictures do have a tremendous feel for the country itself, the atmosphere vividly conveyed in sky, trees, hedges, fields and hills. 'The easy bit is the landscape, the hard part is putting the horsemen in: the scale is so hard,' he says. Where the artist has failed in this, it will be apparent that if the figures are visualised 'three frames on', the riders will be looking through the upstairs window of a house, or otherwise appear disproportionate to the background.

Sir Stephen Furness, as Robin Furness is in private life, has been interested in both painting and hunting all his life.

At school at Charterhouse, he was lucky enough to be taught by Ian Fleming-Williams, an excellent teacher and leading expert on Constable. 'I've always been interested, particularly in light. Light to me is the fascination, particularly of landscape paintings.' Good teaching at school enabled him to express this enthusiasm through the medium of paint. For many years, though, it was not the subtleties of winter light, with which he is now concerned, that absorbed his time, but the brighter, harsher light of other countries.

For on leaving school he went to sea, serving with the Royal Navy and the Fleet Air Arm for ten years. In Malta he was soon producing scenes for tourists, and found a little shop which would sell them for him for three pounds, enough for 'a jolly good meal and a run ashore.' He comes of a family with strong hunting connections and on leaving the Navy in 1962, a year after his marriage to his wife Mary, who is an excellent horsewoman, they moved to a farm in County Durham and started hunting with the Braes of Derwent. He is now farming in North Yorkshire with his son and hunting with the Bedale. He was Master there from 1979 to 1987, and his 230 acre farm still retains, because of hunting, the lovely thorn hedges planted in 1871.

At first he was too busy learning to farm to have much time for painting, but he had long been an admirer of such great sporting artists as Lionel Edwards and Peter Biegel, and was soon striving to follow in their footsteps. Whilst to his regret he never met Lionel Edwards, a big exhibition of sporting paintings on Exmoor gave him the opportunity not only to sell three or four of his own early paintings but also to meet Peter Biegel.

Robin Furness in his studio. (*Farmers Weekly: Reed Farmers Publishing Group*)

The real turning point in his professional life came in 1968, at the Country Fair at Wynyard, near his home. Friends persuaded him that he should exhibit, so he took a large tent, twenty by ten, then found himself struggling to fill such an enormous area. In his effort to produce the quantity, quality inevitably suffered, but, with prices around fifteen pounds, he sold a number. Much more important than his sales was the discovery that amongst the visitors to his tent was the great North Country hunting artist Tom Carr. An introduction was soon arranged; Robin Furness later wrote of that day: 'I first met Tom Carr – the best thing that ever happened.'

Tom Carr was 'not a man to interfere', but he was persuaded to take the exhibitor round every picture and tell him what he thought. 'I learnt more that afternoon . . .' but that was only the beginning. Tom Carr became a close friend and mentor. Sometimes they would work together on a picture, which provided a wonderful opportunity for learning from him.

As well as the technicalities, there were many 'wrinkles to painting out of doors, such as standing on two fertiliser bags so your feet don't get cold and not painting for more than two hours because the light has changed.'

Whilst the details of a picture can be completed in the studio afterwards, the real work is done out of doors, and at some speed because of the constantly changing nature of light and weather. Further sketches and notes made at the time can be worked on later, though where possible Robin Furness likes to use his original landscape. Like most artists painting animals, he uses Muybridge's book of photographs of animals in every conceivable position. Occasionally a dressage expert will suggest that a particular position is impossible, but there is always a photograph to confirm it.

Most of his work today is done on commission, which virtually guarantees a sale (he has only three times had commission work rejected: all subsequently sold, one, unrecognised, to the wife of the person who originally commissioned it). But 'hunting people often want a coloured photograph, they don't want a picture.' They also 'tend to go for pretty bits of landscape, which is rarely best: hunting has to look natural.' Some also demand oils, thinking this is a better investment, but the detailed accuracy required by most hunting people is achieved better in gouache. Scenes which include some four or five horsemen are usually more effective than those incorporating the whole field. Large numbers of figures also make a picture more expensive because it is more time consuming. Robin Furness still tends to find hounds more difficult than horses, though he is overcoming this by practising on the puppies he walks.

Where a picture is to be made into a print, there is a tendency to 'lose definition: you have to overcook it.' In partnership with David Grayling, he has finished a set of six prints of the different fell packs, which have been issued at yearly intervals. Hunts too may commission a print, but only a limited number of countries will be able to sell enough to justify the print run.

Whenever Robin Furness is out in the country, he always has a small sketch book in his pocket, ready to capture a sky, what the poet Will Ogilvy called 'a gleam of November sun' or, just occasionally, a glimpse of a fox or perhaps cubs playing. Then he will forget his commission work and have the basis for something different, for, as he says, 'real hunting people love a painting of a fox.'

23

THE SADDLER

Sydney Free

Sydney Free is one of the very few saddlers remaining in Britain who still makes his own saddles and bridlework. Nothing is too much trouble for him and he retains the standards of an earlier generation. Yet it was only by chance that he came into the trade at all. As a young man he started working on a farm in Norfolk but a partial deformity of his feet made this an unsatisfactory occupation for him. He was sent on a six-month course for assessment to find the most suitable calling. Metalwork was medically inappropriate, but he came out at the top of the leatherwork section. After a further six months on an industrial course, arrangements were made for him to be apprenticed to W. G. Hayes, the saddlers of Cirencester. It was some time later that Sydney discovered that his great great grandfather had been in the saddlery trade. The original skills had come out after four generations, and had been recognised.

He remained with Hayes for twenty-one years, rising to become their foreman. Difficulties then started to beset the firm, and he eventually left to set up on his own in 1974. His Cirencester shop is a thriving business, but he leaves the running of that to his stepson, for, as he says, 'a Master Saddler has got to be at the bench turning the work out.' However, when customers come in to discuss a problem with a saddle, he sees them himself and can generally tell straight away what is causing the difficulty.

He feels that horse people have changed since the early fifties. Saddlers today 'can get away with blue murder', taking short cuts which reduce initial costs but frequently prove a false economy and can occasionally be dangerous. On bridlework, for example, one criterion of quality and durability is the number of stitches to the inch. Where once Sydney Free would have done eleven stitches, today for reasons of economy he will more often do nine, or eight for headcollars. Other firms will reduce much further, to eight or seven, and sometimes six for headcollars. He always uses pigskin for the seats of saddles, which is hard to obtain but lasts a lifetime, whereas the more widely used hide can wear out in six or seven years.

Another important influence on customers is convenience. The Cirencester shop stocks the popular modern synthetic girths which may be machine washed, though its owner points out to customers prepared to listen that these do occasionally snap. His own leather girths – he particularly favours the

Atherstone pattern – incorporate a strengthening strip as well as an oiled cloth to keep them supple. He also recommends lining saddles with serge, when no numnah is required, though he does encourage the use of real sheepskin or cotton numnahs even with correctly fitted leather lined saddles today, for some aspect of the modern tanning process for leather can cause a horse's back to blister.

Other problems arise from the difficulty in obtaining parts and materials, many of which are imported, of an adequate standard. On the roundings on a

Sydney Free at work on a saddle. (*Moments Calendars Ltd, Birmingham*)

Pelham bit, for example, buckles are preferable to hook studs, many of which are faulty.

When making a saddle, Sydney Free fits it both to the rider and the horse, but 'the horse comes first with me because he is dumb and cannot say what's pinching him.' He goes out to hunting yards for alterations during the season, working on the tack room table, to ensure that the horse is comfortable with the finished product. Recently, though, when asked to adjust a polo pony's saddle, he found its withers so damaged that he threatened to call the RSPCA unless it was rested immediately. He is not an adherent of the spring tree, for, although it is more comfortable for the rider, it tends to press down in the middle whilst a rigid tree stays in the right place. This is particularly important with hunters when the saddle is worn for long hours. Similarly, riders often prefer a saddle which is too long in the seat for the comfort of the horse.

Most modern saddles are made on a production line. Sydney Free's saddles and bridlework are all hand sewn, which makes them more expensive: where a mass-produced saddle might cost £300 his will be £575. With the materials costing £200 and 42 hours' work involved this is good value; an hourly rate comparable to that charged by garages would put the cost at around £900. A bridle takes up to 10 hours and the leather costs 80p an ounce.

For a new saddle, Sydney Free first makes a template of the horse's back. He also likes to see the rider's seat on a horse and, without commenting, will then make allowances for any irregularities. Almost everyone (even if left handed) puts more weight on the offside. This stirrup bar particularly should therefore be checked on old saddles, and he will put additional padding on the offside to allow for this. He is then able to make the saddle in the style chosen by the rider to be as comfortable as possible for both rider and horse.

He is one of perhaps only four saddlers still able to repair side saddles, where both the fit and the rider's seat are particularly important, and can give much help to inexperienced customers. Most repair work constitutes a service rather than a profitable business.

Sydney Free also plays a part in the training of young saddlers, not only with his own apprentices but as a judge in the City and Guilds saddlery examinations, where a high standard is maintained. Today, there are more girls than men coming into the trade, and many men leave even after they have qualified. The apprenticeship is four years: it used to be five, but less has now to be learnt on the harness side. Sydney Free himself learned every aspect, including black harness, which is never worked on regularly by the same saddler as brown harness, and excluding only collar making, which is a trade on its own.

Cirencester is an excellent centre for a saddler catering for the top end of the market: many leading hunting, eventing and polo playing families live in or near Gloucestershire. Sydney Free's customers cover a much wider area, from North Wales to East Anglia, and down to the south coast. The assessor who first spotted his potential showed remarkable judgment.

24

THE PUPPY WALKER
Mrs Kath Haynes

Hound puppies have always been sent out to walk, although Peter Beckford, writing in 1781, had reservations about the system 'greatly owing, I believe, to the little care that is taken of them there. I am in doubt whether it might not be better to breed them up yourself, and have a kennel on purpose.' A century later, J. Otho Paget, editing his work, declared 'This has been proved impossible. Hounds to be reared successfully must go out to walk . . . (those) that survive the dangers of walks always appear to have more sense than those that are kept at home.'

Today, puppies are usually only sent to people who are prepared to take trouble with them. The standard of puppy walking is high, yet there can be few more successful puppy walkers than Mrs Haynes, in the Heythrop country. She has now walked more than sixty couple of puppies, missing only two years since she started in 1956, and frequently having as many as three couples in a year. She first started walking puppies when Captain Wallace persuaded her to take a day-old puppy and bottle feed it. She reared it successfully, keeping it warm with a hot water bottle and the puppy stayed with her until it was six months old. 'I upset myself when he did go back,' but 'he wasn't a scrap of good; he wouldn't hunt. As soon as he saw me that was it: he wanted to come home.'

Undeterred, she took day-old puppies to bottle feed for two more years, since when she has taken them at weaning. The experience with the hand reared puppies stood her in good stead later when one couple developed jaundice and she successfully nursed them through it, bottle feeding them on broth. She used to take them out on collars and leads, which benefits the puppies when they return to kennels and are coupled to older hounds. Now that she is getting older, they are mostly left with the run of her garden, and shut in only if she is out for a long time, in case they should somehow accidentally be let out or escape. A century ago the main risk to puppies at walk came from distemper. Today they are inoculated but face worse dangers on the roads. Although she no longer takes them out, she does spend much time with them: 'they get fussed a lot, and they know me when they go back to the kennels.'

Mrs Haynes has passed on her enthusiasm for hounds to her son George, who has been kennel huntsman of the RAC beagles at Cirencester since 1965. Her

Mrs Kath Haynes in the show ring at Peterborough with Captain R. E. Wallace, MFH, Anthony Adams and Heythrop Fairytale, Hearsay, Headline and Helmet. (*Jim Meads*)

husband (formerly stud groom at Buttermilk where the outstanding race horses Park Top and Spartan General were both bred) also gave her great support.

Mrs Haynes prefers to take bitches since her own terriers, who have been used to puppies all their lives, are bitches. This also means that she is able to walk successive generations of the same family, taking puppies from the litters of bitches she has walked, although many of them will be sired by dogs from different packs.

An important date in every puppy walker's diary is the Puppy Show, which is the Masters' opportunity to thank them. This generally takes place in June, when most of the puppies are rather over a year old, and have probably been back in kennels for some months. The length of time for which puppies stay at walk varies, but Mrs Haynes tends to take hers at six to eight weeks old and keep them until they are about six months.

Two distinguished judges are generally invited in from elsewhere. Whilst a puppy walker can do little to influence a hound's conformation, proper feeding and exercise will clearly aid its development and the way it shows itself will owe much to the way it has been handled at walk. Mrs Haynes has a large cupboard tightly packed with trophies won by her hounds at the Puppy Show. The tea afterwards, with the judges' speeches and the presentation of prizes, is always a memorable occasion.

Most successful on the flags of all Mrs Haynes' puppies was Hearsay, whom Mrs Haynes walked, together with her two litter sisters Helmet and Headline. They were all out of Paper, whom Mrs Haynes had also walked. This couple and a half were matched up with a fourth bitch, Fairytale, who was from a different litter and had been walked by someone else, but who closely resembled them, and together they won the two couple class at Peterborough. Later that afternoon Hearsay went on to become Reserve Champion Bitch.

Mrs Haynes no longer goes to Peterborough: she stopped going during her husband's last illness. She still goes out with hounds in the car every Saturday during the season, and has a marvellous collection of hunting scrap books, which she takes trouble to keep up to date. But, despite all her memorabilia, her best collection of all is not at home but in the Heythrop kennels; all those hounds, or their descendants, who have gone on to excel in the field and sometimes on the flags, thanks to the exceptional start in life which she gave them.

25

THE FELL MASTER

Edmund Porter

Six Fell packs hunt foxes on foot in the hills of the Lake District, probably the most beautiful country in England. Of these, only one is privately owned. The Eskdale and Ennerdale Hounds were left to Mr William Porter, grandfather of the present Master, by their founder, Tommy Dobson, in 1910. Today the full responsibility for these hounds has devolved on Mr Edmund Porter, the third generation of his family to hunt them.

Few packs rely more heavily on a single individual. With no professional help at all, Edmund Porter combines the responsibilities of Master and amateur huntsman with the duties of professional huntsman, whipper-in and kennel-man.

There is not even a regular amateur whipper-in: different followers help when they can. The Master, after whipping in for five seasons, started hunting hounds in 1963, and still carries his grandfather's horn. He takes sole responsibility for every aspect of kennel management, from picking up the flesh to breeding hounds, a field in which he has been particularly successful, as a cupboard full of trophies proves. 'I always reckon to breed for work, and if you come across a show hound, well, you show it. We've had quite a few nice hounds these last few years...'

In the Fell packs traditionally many of the old hounds as well as puppies go out to walk in the summer. This allows the Master a few weeks to work on his own account, when he is often busy building stone walls, and for other ventures. In the summer of 1990 he and his wife were invited to visit the United States to give a series of presentations on Fell fox hunting, taking with them some puppies to join various American packs. Some of the eight presentations required more than five hundred miles' driving in a day, but the interchange of ideas between hunting enthusiasts from both sides of the Atlantic made for some memorable moments.

In Eskdale and Ennerdale country so much is based on tradition. No meet cards are ever sent out, for it is well known locally where hounds will be for any week in the season. The Puppy Show, which includes classes for the best walked entered and unentered hounds, is always held at the King George, the local public house, on the second Saturday in September. Hounds return there from

Edmund Porter, MFH, Master of the Eskdale and Ennerdale Hounds. (*Jim Meads*)

their walks, and go back to kennels that evening. Hunting starts on the following Monday. As hounds have not been regularly exercised, mornings are short at first until fitness is built up.

The same area will be hunted for four days in a week, before hounds move on to the adjoining valley. 'It's a tradition really, which goes back to my grandfather's time. There was no transport in those days, so they'd set off from kennels the day before they were due to be hunting in a particular area, on bicycles, probably. There'd be two of them then, a huntsman and a whipper-in, and they'd kennel hounds on the farm for a week and make that their headquarters.'

Maize meal would have been delivered to the farm beforehand for hounds, and the huntsman's first job would be to make his pudding. Even today hounds are fed predominantly on pudding, with flesh once a week. 'We've just kept up the same thing, only nowadays we travel from kennels each day. The only places where we stay are Great Langdale and Little Langdale. If we miss one day, we'll go the next: nobody minds.'

The Opening Meet and Boxing Day are at the King George and tend to attract a number of casual visitors. At the end of March and in early April, hunting men and women whose own seasons have finished converge on the Lake District. Regular fixtures finish at Easter, whenever that may fall, and after that hounds go out on lambing call. Some meets, inevitably, are more popular than others, though not necessarily with the Master. 'I love being out on my own: you can concentrate on your work then, on what your hounds are doing and such like.'

Whilst his country is less plagued with busy roads than is much of the Lake District, he feels that it has altered greatly, including much afforestation. Fortunately, this is mostly in small parcels. 'It is more difficult to hunt hounds in big woodlands, especially if it's windy. I hate wind: you can't hear hounds working and they can't hear the horn.'

Despite some changes, hunting in this country is carried on much as it was in Edmund Porter's grandfather's time. Many of the farms where hounds are walked remain unchanged. Even the hounds' names are the same: when an old hound dies, his or her successor at that farm will be given the same name. If Thomas Dobson, who first became Master in 1857, could return to Cumbria, he would find remarkably little change. He would know where to find hounds in any given week, even though the kennels are now better situated, and he would feel well pleased with the way the Porter family had looked after its legacy.

26

THE HUNTING DOCTOR

Dr Tom Connors

There are few better known or liked characters in the hunting world than Tom Connors. An Irishman who has practised as a doctor in Leicester-shire since 1949, and a superb horseman, he is also an outstandingly successful dealer. Everyone in the Shires knows or knows of him, many of the best horses are supplied by him.

Things were different in 1949 when he arrived, newly qualified, from his home in Ireland to take up a position with the medical practice in Long Clawson where he is now senior partner. He chose the area for the hunting – 'If I'm coming to England I'm coming to Leicestershire or Gloucestershire' – but his first ever day with the Quorn, cubhunting at Ella's Gorse, did not start auspiciously.

After killing a brace and a half, they let hounds go. The young doctor was riding a five year old which had been up all summer, had won the five year old Heavyweight class at Dublin and was extremely fit. Used to hunting with the Waterford, where Dick Russell, the great amateur huntsman, was happy to have the hard riding members of his small field close behind him provided they kept out of his way, Tom Connors had no conception of the role of a Leicester-shire Field Master. He was close behind George Barker, the huntsman, when there was a roar from the Field Master. 'What the ... ... do you think you're doing? Trying to jump on hounds?'

The young man knew no-one. 'I thought, "If this is hunting in England, I think I'm going to give it up."' But Denis Aldridge, the sporting artist who later became Quorn Hunt Secretary, saw the position very clearly and reassured him. Shortly afterwards the Field Master had a fall. 'I jumped off and went and saw that he was all right, and I said "By the way, sir, I'm sorry. I wasn't trying to jump on your hounds."'

'"Did I say that? Forget about it." He had a few stops then and I gave him a lead. We were friends ever after.'

Even before that first day, he had had some hunting patients. Some came to the surgery, which was not then effectively sound-proofed. An old earth stopper soon forgot his ailments to talk of the exploits of the former Prince of Wales, describing a fence jumped by him alone. The door opened to reveal the indignant figure of Sir Gilbert Greenall's second horseman. 'You're wrong. It was two hundred yards further down.' Others he found when officially off duty. At a hunter trial, a request was made over the loud speaker for him to go the car park. The Belvoir huntsman, George Tonge, saw a farmer whom he did not wish to miss as he arrived in the car park.

Jumping out quickly, he inadvertently slammed the door on his passenger's fingers. Enraged, the passenger concluded that it had been done intentionally by an old breeches maker who happened to be standing there, and promptly laid him out. The doctor arrived to hear the old man murmuring 'It wasn't I who hit him at all'.

One frosty morning he found himself helping a respected elderly General to attend to someone concussed when his horse had slipped up and come down. Having sent for a tractor, Dr Connors noticed the General's worried look. 'Young man, I don't like the look of this fellow at all. I wish to God we had a doctor.' He replied meekly 'I'm afraid I'm a doctor.'

He can quickly distinguish between serious cases and those who are merely hysterical, when 'you have got to treat them a little bit rough.' With one young girl who was screaming and kicking her legs, he told her firmly to sit up, then stand up, then lead the pony on to the road. She obeyed him, but a watching friend of his was appalled. 'When I get a fall I want better treatment than that. I don't want to be told to stand up.'

He emphasises that the first priority when someone has had a bad fall is to ensure that they have a clear airway. If they are unconscious, it is easier to ensure this if they are turned on one side, though if there is any question of damage to the back they must be kept straight when being turned. The other vital factor is speed, particularly in cases of internal injury. Whoever telephones for the ambulance should arrange to meet it at some well known, unmistakeable land mark and guide it from there to avoid delay. He long ago arranged for the fencing vehicle to carry a stretcher. When one patient unfortunately sank through the original one, he had it replaced with a better, scoop type stretcher. He now advocates that the fencing party should also be equipped with a mobile telephone. He carries in his own pocket morphia, pain killing tablets and a few bandages.

The need for fast action was demonstrated when a girl had a serious fall immediately in front of him. Dr Connors saw that she had stopped breathing, but by giving her mouth-to-mouth resuscitation and arranging for someone else to massage her chest at the same time, he succeeded in restoring her breathing until oxygen was available, and stayed with her until she was being suitably cared for in hospital.

For many years, Tom Connors would see patients both before and after hunting, and, when he first came, take all the night calls as well to make time to hunt. 'Good hunting people would never say that they hadn't got the time to hunt.' Today, as senior partner, he usually arranges a full day off on hunting days. When he first came, he kept three horses, did them himself, and hacked them almost everywhere, soon making so many friends amongst the farming

Dr Tom Connors: away from Ella's Gorse with the Quorn. (*Jim Meads*)

fraternity that he could school over much of the land he rode through. He is also a great believer in schooling horses over cross country fences on the lunge.

He soon realised that 'I wouldn't be able to ride good horses if I weren't doing a bit of dealing.' Besides, 'horses and dealing are a disease – once you're in it it's impossible to get out of it.' So he somehow finds time for regular visits to Ireland to find horses, which he now insists must have been properly hunted, or to see those found for him by his brother there, and then to oversee their schooling before showing them to potential buyers.

Tom Connors would be sorely missed by hunting people in the Shires. All enjoy his company, many are indebted to him for the best horses they have ever owned, and a few for their lives.

27

A MEMBER OF THE FIELD –
THE BUILDER

Wilf Gamble

'I broke one in myself and used to yoke him in the cart. Then I bought a bigger one and broke him in and started hunting on him.' This was Jimmy, who, whilst bigger than his predecessor, still measures only 14 hands 2 inches. Fourteen years later, Wilf Gamble is still hunting him regularly with the Sinnington in Yorkshire.

Wilf was not brought up with horses, although, like many country boys of his generation, he rode if ever a chance arose. 'I've never been taught to ride you know.' One of a family of thirteen, he has worked hard all his life, and combining the care of his horses with his work as a builder requires considerable dedication. For it is no longer only Jimmy. After his arrival, 'I bought one for my son, then bought another one for my daughter. Three takes some doing.' Whilst he only had three for one season, during which one of his two loose boxes had to be partitioned in two, he has generally had two horses in since that time. Tragically, his son, who had been jumping gates with the Sinnington at the age of fifteen, later joined the RAF and was killed in an accident. Wilf did not hunt at all during the following season: 'You can't go half-hearted.' But since then he has found that hunting is 'the only thing that takes my mind off it.'

Doing two horses is time-consuming. 'I go to work at half past seven, see, and finish at four-thirty or five.' This means he must be up at six each morning, and in the evening he returns to the stables as soon as he has had his dinner, without sitting down. He exercises in a field in the dark. Extra chores like clipping have somehow to be fitted in. Nor can he rest after the season is over, for he must compensate for working time spent hunting, 'I work a lot of hours during the summer.' But Wilf has no regrets. 'It's something that gets hold of you, isn't it? You can't give it up.'

Non-hunting friends tease him about the cost, but 'Really in a sense it doesn't cost me a lot. You don't buy everything all at once. The wife bought me a jacket at Christmas. I do a bit of hay carting and I get a bit of hay. I feed a bit of barley you know. I did some draining for one chap – when he was combining his barley I backed up to the combine.' He also has a great friend who is a blacksmith and they manage to help each other. His daughter can also sometimes help, for she is training to be a veterinary nurse. He owns three and a half acres and rents three further fields, where he keeps a few sheep and cattle as well as grazing the two horses there in summer.

When Wilf first started hunting, he subscribed to the Farndale, which is more of a moorland country. At that time, he was happy to complete a day without a fall, and it was a good country for watching hounds work. But 'I won't by-pass nothing now, I just sit back and kick at him,' and he finds hunting with the Sinnington from his home in the best of their country, close to the kennels, most convenient. Sometimes it enables him to have a second horse: 'If the meet's this side, I'll slip back and change over.' On other occasions, he accepts a lift back to kennels with the Hunt first horses when they change. He hunts every Wednesday, but only occasional Saturdays, for he enjoys shooting also. If he has a spare

Wilf Gamble with Jimmy. (*James Buxton*)

horse and his daughter is not able to hunt, he will gladly mount one of his friends.

It is not just the sporting side which appeals to Wilf. 'I enjoy the hunt balls. I enjoy all the social side. I get too much to drink and I get into a bit of mischief. You can get carried away sometimes, can't you?' On one memorable hunting morning, Wilf was too busy to have time for breakfast. An over-hospitable host pressed four or five whiskies on him at the meet. 'All of a sudden I fell off sideways, flat on my back.' He was helped back on, but 'I fell off again and rolled down the hillside. I was only riding me little 'orse but I couldn't get back on. People said as I fell off three times, but it was only twice. I couldn't get back on.' Since then he has learnt his lesson: he never misses breakfast.

He is always ready to help the Hunt or Pony Club, of which his daughter was a keen member, in any practical way he can. He will gladly take on such jobs as levelling sand over the road crossings at the point-to-point, 'but you won't get me on to the Committee.'

Hunting to Wilf is 'something that gets hold of you. You can't give it up. If you've got to do it, you've got to do it.'

28

THE HUNT SECRETARY

Dick Watson

'One's got to be rather like a dentist: extract the right article and leave the patient fairly happy at the end of it all' is how Dick Watson sums up the work of a Hunt Secretary. When he retired recently after forty-eight seasons as Honorary Secretary of the Fernie, he had achieved just that. Everyone paid their fair share, yet the secretary remained the best liked and most respected man in the country. Now in his mid-eighties, he continues to hunt two days a week, immaculately turned out and often giving the younger generation a lead across the Leicestershire fences.

He first took on the secretaryship during the War, when he was 'a very junior member of the Finance Committee'. Money was short and the Hunt could no longer afford to pay a secretary. At the time, it was not a big job, for there were few people hunting, and only a handful of subscriptions to collect, whilst today there will be close to three hundred. Turnover during the same period has increased almost forty fold. Having been brought up in the country and hunted from childhood, he had no difficulty in knowing everybody. From this base, he has been able to learn the new names and faces gradually, as numbers have escalated. He feels great sympathy for those coming new to the job today in a popular country.

As senior partner in a leading local firm of solicitors for many years, he found the office back-up to which he had access of immense value. But most important of all he rates 'a helpful wife.' His wife Joan hunted on a horse for the first two decades of his secretaryship, and in a Land Rover for the remaining thirty years. He found 'the different aspects of everything that you get most interesting, and most helpful too. On a horse, we heard the same things, but on wheels (you are talking to) quite a different cross section of people.'

Endless patience also is demanded of the Hunt Secretary's wife or husband, for both telephone calls and personal visits are unceasing. The callers have a wide range of different times for eating, and few make allowance for those to which the secretary and his family wish to adhere. He is also expected to be a mine of information on every topic, from sartorial questions to weather fore-casting. Complete strangers will ring to enquire about a particular horse. With up to 150 out in a day, 'you can't really know anything about them. You go hunting to watch hounds, apart from being secretary and watching your field.'

One query which particularly delighted Dick Watson came from a middle aged lady dragged into his yard 'by a rather noisy spaniel on a lead, barking and jumping about. "I can't do anything with this dog. Would you have it to hunt with your dogs?" ' All his legendary tact and charm were required to persuade her to remove it without taking offence.

These qualities are particularly necessary when collecting money. 'You have got to collect the right amount obviously. Sometimes they think that they might have been asked for a bit more than you were satisfied with. With the majority of them you make them feel fairly important as part of the game really. The more important they feel, the more generous they are, and if they are not generous it doesn't do some of them any harm just to be told so, and explain that they've got to pay their share.' When they pay also matters, for expenses continue throughout the summer. A small incentive such as a free meet card for payment perhaps by the 1st September can prove worthwhile. Excuses have changed little over the years: cheques continue to be left on the kitchen table and cheque books finished with monotonous regularity. Even so, 'For thirty odd years I'd never been done down for a cap' (payment for a single day rather than a subscription for regular hunting) until the record was broken by a foreigner who could not be traced.

On Opening Meet day in the past the secretary might be handed coins totalling perhaps ten pounds. Today notes and cheques come to thousands of pounds. Many will be thoughtlessly handed over without identification. Dick Watson would use as many as eight different pockets, and train his memory to link each with a particular person. On every day's hunting it is essential for the secretary to see exactly who is out and know which of these must be asked for money. 'Your horse wants to be mannerly. I was always the first to arrive at the meet. It's amazing how easily you do spot late comers even with a big field. It's all a matter of training.' When he first started, everyone paid field money each time they came out. Then regular subscribers were allowed to compound this into a lump sum, and subsequently it was merged with the subscription, and the burden on the secretary was reduced. Today, visitors are expected to ask before coming out, and on a fashionable day the need to restrict the size of fields may necessitate turning some people away. It is therefore wise to ask well in advance, but considerate to confirm or cancel plans nearer the day, so that if a visitor will not after all be able to hunt, his place may be offered to another.

'You've got to have a fairly placid nature, because you do get people who could make you extremely angry. The great thing is to sleep on it, but you've got to be prepared to spark when necessary.' If an irate farmer rings up, 'it's completely useless entering into an argument: talk about something entirely different. They usually mellow after a while.' In an extreme case many years ago, Mr Watson recalls accompanying the Master, in some trepidation, on a visit to a farmer who had actually shot a hound. They talked for an hour without mentioning hunting at all and everyone was extremely pleasant.

In the Fernie country, in addition to the Honorary Secretary, there used to be

Dick Watson shaking hands with Diana Stanhope, member of a leading Fernie farming family, at a meet at her home on her 21st birthday.

a paid field secretary who was responsible for the country and the farmers. Today this side is covered by the Masters. In many countries one man combines both functions as a full-time job. Whilst free of this responsibility, Dick Watson did cover much of the financial side, paying all those bills which were not the responsibility of the Masters. Masters are always responsible for the hunt staff, and the relationship between them must never be interfered with by the Secretary nor the Hunt Committee he serves. Masters in the traditional sense are paid a guaranteed sum by the Committee and meet all further expenses from their own pockets. Such an arrangement is rare today, most Masters being Acting Masters who make a contribution but leave the Hunt Committee to carry the unlimited financial responsibility. It will often be left to the Secretary to negotiate the details and workings of all such arrangements.

Many other duties devolve on the Secretary. He will organise the mailing of circulars such as subscription lists, invitations to the Puppy Show or Earthstoppers' Dinner, meet cards and their printing and so on. Despite its voluntary nature, 'it seems a pretty full time job. But it's an interesting job because you get to know what everyone else is doing.'

Usually, when Hunt Secretaries retire, they cease to be members of the Hunt Secretaries Association. Uniquely, Dick Watson was appointed a life member and asked to remain on the Committee. When the Chairman was unable to attend recently, he stepped into his shoes. 'I reckon I got the meeting through in double quick time too!' But then, if you are used to fitting two major jobs into your life without ever appearing to be in a rush, and always having time for everybody, that is to be expected.

29

THE GAMEKEEPER

Kieron Moore

The Gamekeeper may seem an unlikely character to appear in a hunting book in any role save that of villain. But Kieron Moore, head keeper on Lord de Ramsey's Abbots Ripton estate near Huntingdon, is proving himself a hero to the Fitzwilliam Hunt. For eighteen years this part of the country had not been hunted, but hounds have now regularly been drawing the Abbots Ripton coverts, and finding and killing foxes. The head keeper delights in this, only finding it frustrating on those occasions when hounds are unable to kill their fox. He is even considering keeping a horse.

Kieron Moore's philosophy of 'Live and Let Live' is an indication that his approach is different from that of many of his calling. Yet there is nothing unusual in his background.

He first came to the estate as a boy of sixteen in 1974 and learnt his trade under a head keeper of the old school. 'It was drummed into me that all foxes and vermin have got to go,' he recalls. Six years later he was given a part of the estate to take charge of single handed. He operated this on traditional lines. After a further six years the whole estate was once again brought together as a single unit. Kieron Moore became head keeper, with three under keepers, two of whom were older than him.

During his first twelve months 257 foxes were killed on the estate. Shortly afterwards, James Barclay, a Joint Master of the Fitzwilliam, came to see him. At first, he says 'I took a lot of convincing': it would have been remarkable had this not been the case, for 'I had been brought up to kill foxes.' For another year he remained 'very active in fox control'. Yet much of what the Master was saying to him fitted in with what he had already been thinking. For Kieron is a highly intelligent man with a passionate belief in the country, in field sports and in conservation: few keepers would welcome, as he does, a pair of buzzards on the estate. Despite natural scepticism from some of his team, he gave up the destruction of foxes. Since then the number of foxes killed on the estate by him or his underkeepers can be counted on the fingers of one hand. Fox control is left to the Fitzwilliam Hounds.

The results have been remarkable. It is now evident that the old policy of destruction resulted in more and more foxes coming on to the estate from the surrounding countryside. Now that there is a resident fox population, interlopers

Kieron Moore with his dog. (*James Buxton*)

are kept at bay by their own kind. Previously, considerable time and money was devoted by the estate to the destruction of foxes. Regular night drives with lamps for shooting foxes and the checking twice daily of enormous numbers of snares were time consuming for the keepers. Now much of this is saved, though extra trouble is taken over ensuring the security of the pens where the English partridges are reared. Careful work on maintenance of wire netting and the use of fox-repellent chemicals does much to ensure protection. Further measures are currently under consideration. Kieron admits that an occasional rogue fox may have to be destroyed, but it is not a frequent problem.

The new approach on the estate has the full support of Lord de Ramsey, a previous Master of the Fitzwilliam, whose daughter-in-law, the Hon. Mrs John Fellowes, hunts regularly with the Fitzwilliam. In a recent experiment, hounds were invited to hunt on the estate just two days before a shooting day. There was appalling weather on both occasions, and the hunting day unfortunately was the only disappointing one hounds had on the estate all season. But on the shooting day, less than forty-eight hours after hounds had drawn the coverts, not only was there an excellent bag but it was generally agreed that birds were flying better than usual, when conditions were such that the opposite might have been expected.

Whether from Kieron's example or because they have reached similar con-clusions independently, other keepers are beginning to think on similar lines. Kieron himself is a great believer in communication. He welcomes groups of visitors to the estate for the chance they give him to explain his point of view to a wider audience. Even trespassers receive a polite explanation of the disturbance to wildlife caused by them and their dogs. Keepers who would shoot a stray dog not only appal him but strike him as remarkably short-sighted: 'They are giving everybody a bad name and making a rod for their own backs: they will find themselves out of a job.' Such behaviour, he feels, will lead to the abolition of field sports, just as, if hunting goes, shooting will surely follow. 'We're all in this situation together. Nobody's sport wants to disappear: we've got to help and support each other.'

30

THE FOOT FOLLOWER
Jimmy Gutch

'These hounds – the ultimate is in the moonlight. When you hear them in the dark it's out of this world.' The hounds in question are the glorious big, black and tan Dumfriesshire foxhounds, which hunt the country around Lockerbie in Scotland. Jimmy Gutch has been following them, on foot and in the car, ever since he moved to the area soon after the war.

He was brought up in the North Warwickshire country in a world where following hounds was taken for granted. Not only his parents but most of the boys in the district came out.

Even then, he must have been keener than his contemporaries, for the huntsman of the North Warwickshire offered him a job in kennels, but then the war came. For three and a half years of it he was a prisoner in Malaya, and 'I never thought there'd be any hunting after that.' When he eventually came home, 'you could see which way things were going.' Sadly, his forecast was correct. The North Warwickshire had been a four day a week country before the war: it was disbanded because of increasing urbanisation in 1985.

So he moved instead to Dumfriesshire, and trained there as a forester, favouring the less densely populated area. He regards population control as the vital issue for conservation: 'It was not otter-hunting that put the otter away, just people. They never had any peace in the river.' The Dumfriesshire is a marvellous hunting country, both to ride across and in which to follow hounds on foot. The estates of the Master, Sir Rupert Buchanan-Jardine, comprise a large proportion of the country, with gates which open easily everywhere, as well as jumpable fences and no plough. The hills offer many commanding positions from which to watch hounds work, and these hounds, with their wonderful cry, can be listened to as they hunt through the woodland country. For Jimmy Gutch, a quiet, gentle countryman, now retired, walking with field glasses to some vantage point amongst the hills, then using his car for the longer distances, you can 'definitely see the best of it.' The dark hounds show up on the grass, to his mind more clearly than a muddy light coloured hound, and they can be heard all the time. Their cry means that it is most unusual for them to 'chop' a fox, which is unlikely to be caught unawares whilst asleep.

He feels that hunting people are very privileged. 'You get access to places where you'd never go in your lifetime if it weren't for hunting. That's why it's so vital not to abuse it.' He does not feel that hunting people are sufficiently appreciative: 'I think they're thoroughly spoilt up here by Sir Rupert. They don't know how lucky they are.' No car cap is taken; car followers pay £3 a season to belong to the Supporters' Club. 'It's the best £3 you could imagine, but some do not even pay that, and they have the impudence to grumble!'

Jimmy Gutch himself finds many ways in which to help, though he dismisses the hours he puts in tidying up and painting at the kennels with the comment that 'we're not subscribers, we owe a great debt to hunting and I think we should do a bit.' Nor would he mention the hounds there that owe their lives to him, for at the end of the day's sport, he stays to help make sure every hound is safely back: 'I've no horse to put away so I can stay out.' He can thus help to see that no hound is left out, perhaps on the wrong side of a dangerous main road, or, on one occasion, caught up in wire, where he heard and rescued it.

His primary interest is in hounds: 'Horses make a lovely spectacle, but you

Jimmy Gutch with some of the Dumfriesshire Hounds. (*Meriel Buxton*)

wouldn't go just to see the horses, or I wouldn't.' On the other hand, he prefers to hunt with a mounted pack. 'Some foot packs can be lacking a bit in discipline. You don't want all and sundry holloaing. You've got to see that it doesn't become a rabble. A man on a horse can control people.' He is relieved to know that the terrier work is controlled by a single responsible keeper from Sir Rupert's estate, for 'you have got to have very strict discipline with terriers. It can very easily go wrong.'

Jimmy Gutch regrets that he did not have more hunting with the Fell packs when he was younger, although he continues to enjoy a few days every season with them. The inevitable urbanisation of the country concerns him for the future of hunting, as does the scant number of young people in the area showing enthusiasm for the sport. But for him himself the Dumfriesshire have proved a wonderful pack to follow. 'You never get a bad day here: on a poor scent hounds will still speak. As long as they're hunting, by and large you'll hear them.'

31

THE LARGE LANDOWNER
Count Guy de Pelet

'In my opinion, the landowner is the most important person in the hunt because without him there could be no hunting. The Master can change his huntsman, produce a fresh pack of hounds, he can produce foxes, but without the co-operation and consent of the landowner all these efforts would be in vain.'

Count Guy de Pelet is well able to assess the importance of the landowner to hunting, having wide experience of both sides. He has owned the several thousand acre Inwood Estate in the Blackmore Vale country for many years and managed a 'Home Farm' in both bad and more prosperous times for farming. He was Master of the Blackmore Vale from 1959 until 1974. From 1930 until 1959 he was Field Master and Honorary Secretary of Miss Guest's Hounds and then the Blackmore Vale. He inherited the estate from Miss Guest. She and her father, Mr Merthyr Guest, were Masters of Hounds for all but seven years from 1884 to 1960. Count de Pelet's son is now Chairman of the Blackmore and Sparkford Vale.

The Inwood Estate is not only a foxhunter's dream to ride over. The house is almost a hunting museum. The kennels and stables remain, though they no longer house thirty of the more than sixty horses, all grey, and over one hundred couple of hounds, kept by Mr Guest who hunted the country six days a week at his own expense. Many fascinating mementoes of hunting in previous generations are preserved; there is a remarkable collection of hunting horns which once belonged to almost every well known huntsman of the past, from Squire Osbaldeston to the Yellow Earl. Even the terriers are direct descendants of those owned by Parson Jack Russell.

Landowners may be divided into a number of different categories, each with different views and attitudes. First, there is the man or woman 'like myself, long established in the country, who has always had connections with hunting and is therefore favourably disposed.' Such a person may be a great help to the Masters, placing his land at their disposal for hunting, keeping the gateways useable and, as far as is consistent with modern farming methods, taking the wire down, and, where this is not possible, encouraging hunt jumps, as well as keeping his woodlands in good order and the rides well trimmed to facilitate the task of the huntsman when drawing for a fox. In arable countries, he can very often leave headlands.

Then there is the large, often absentee, landowner 'who may have little interest in sport or hunting, or very often a definite interest in shooting.' Unless, perhaps, he has hunted in previous times, his outlook will be quite different, and it will be necessary for the Masters to exercise all their tact to ensure his good will and also that of his gamekeepers or managers.

Thirdly, and most importantly, there is the smaller farmer occupier, dependent on his land for his livelihood. His role, the most crucial of all for hunting, is considered in detail in other chapters, but Count de Pelet emphasises that he must never be hunted over too much so as to appear to cause extensive damage, and it is vital that the Masters keep in close touch with him and see that all repairs are completed as swiftly and efficiently as possible. In the Blackmore Vale country, Count de Pelet feels that this is much more efficiently done than was the case in the past. With a good fence repairing team working from a Land Rover during the day's sport, it is possible for damage to be put right almost instantaneously and that goes a long way to smoothing over any ill feeling caused by possible damage done during the day's sport.

In the case of tenant farmers, it is the duty of the sporting landowner to protect his tenants from over-hunting. He can do this by close personal contacts with the Masters especially when they are in the process of planning their meets. 'When I was Master I tried to avoid hunting over the same farm more than once in three weeks.' Count de Pelet also feels strongly that if a farm has provided good sport in the morning, hounds should try not to return there in the afternoon, when the cows are probably coming in for milking, the farmer is at his busiest, and he will not be keen to find the whole field riding through his yard.

On the other hand, he feels, judging from the Inwood Estate which has been regularly hunted over and farmed for generations, that, provided damage to fences is promptly repaired, damage to grass and crops may appear considerable at the time, but by the spring after chain harrowing and rolling, the affected areas can rarely be distinguished. The provision of easily mended jumping places helps to reduce trouble.

In the past, the landlord had much more control than is the case today. Everything today rests on the existence of a good relationship between landlord and tenant. Whilst old tenancy agreements may still include a proviso requiring the tenant to take down wire, or walk hound puppies, such agreements are clearly unenforceable, and continue to be carried out only through the good will of the tenant. Conversely, rents used to be kept very low, and allowance was made for damage caused by hunting. Today, rents are high and no such allowances are made. Land itself 'is so much more valuable now.'

In the Blackmore Vale country, there are many farmers who hunt or follow hounds. Even so, as a proportion of farmers in a hunting country, the total represents a minority. If fifty farmers hunt in a country, it seems a lot, but one

Count Guy de Pelet out with the Blackmore Vale. (*Jim Meads*)

must bear in mind that there are probably seven or eight hundred farmers in all. However, many who do not hunt themselves, will have some other interest in the sport, following in the car, attending hunt functions, perhaps, or having children who are keen on the Pony Club, often the first step to hunting themselves and giving their parents an interest in the activities of the hunt. Count de Pelet has a Pony Club event course on his land.

There is another respect in which the landowner has less power over hunting than was once the case. In the past, if a major dispute erupted, landowners could lend support to one side or another by attempting, occasionally successfully, to have the boundaries of hunting countries altered. That is no longer possible thanks to the efficient way in which the MFH Association is run. Whilst a landowner today may threaten to ban hounds from his land unless the Master of his choice holds office, no-one with the interests of the sport at heart will do this, for his ultimate sanction is only the banning of hounds from his land absolutely: he can no longer make his land available to a different pack or a different regime.

Large estates in the ownership of men like Count de Pelet reduce the burden of the Masters, for such a landowner will take over many of the duties which elsewhere fall to the Masters. Estates run as Inwood is, with well maintained fences and gateways, are a pleasure for hunting men and women to ride across. Every member of the field can help the cause of hunting by remembering that he is always a guest on the land he hunts over and behaving as such. One gate left open, one fence unnecessarily broken, or one seed field ridden across can cause lasting ill will. Farmers and landowners deserve courtesy and consideration: without them hunting would cease.

'In my experience regard for the owner occupier of the land is, as a general rule, shown by the vast majority of the hunting fraternity and especially by those in authority: there may be at times unfortunate incidents but one must allow for the excitement and thrill of the chase after the hounds.'

32

THE HUNTSMAN'S WIFE
Mrs Tom Normington

'Unless you actually live at the kennels and know what the phone's like, I think people don't realise', remarked Mrs Tom Normington, wife of the huntsman of the Grafton. In many countries, the huntsman's wife is out all day, perhaps doing a job of her own, or on hunting days out with hounds herself, either mounted or in a car. Yet it is precisely on hunting days that the need for somebody at home to take messages is greatest. 'Last Tuesday a couple of gates had been smashed. The farmer wanted them doing that afternoon. I had to catch the box on its way in and send a message.' If that farmer had received no reply from secretary or Masters, who were no doubt all out hunting, and on ringing the kennels had only succeeded in contacting an answerphone, he might have been considering banning hounds from his land by nightfall. Besides, many of the older farmers are reluctant to leave a message on a machine and will simply ring off.

Even where the problem is not caused by the hunt, prompt service makes all the difference. If the kennelman can remove a dead bullock on the same day, its owner will appreciate it. Similarly, when a visitor's horse unfortunately dropped dead during a day's hunting, it could not be left by the roadside. Mrs Normington passes on the messages, then with her knowledge of the country she can help the young kennelman to plan his route for collecting the flesh so as to waste as little time as possible.

Before her marriage, Mrs Normington says 'I was hardly aware of the existence of the hunting world. I didn't have an awful lot of idea of what it was about.' Her father had been brought up in the country, living not far from her present home at the Grafton kennels, near Towcester. The family were living in Peterborough when she first met Tom, at a Farmers' Dance which neither had been keen to attend. She was working as a secretary and feels now that she has let her training go.

Even though she no longer uses a typewriter, it is unlikely that anyone in the Grafton country would agree with her on this point. As well as dealing with incoming calls, she orders the diesel, contacts garages, makes appointments with the vet and so on. She used also to write the cards advising farmers when hounds were likely to cross their land, but lack of time made her ask for other arrangements to be made.

Ann Normington at the Grafton Kennels. (*James Buxton*)

Mrs Normington considers that she has been lucky in having had fewer moves to contend with than many huntsmen's wives. At the time of their marriage, Tom became First Whipper-in to the Grafton. Three years later, he was offered the kennel huntsman's job with the Tynedale, where he stayed seven seasons before returning to the Grafton as huntsman. At this time (1972) their three sons were aged seven, five and three, so there have been no problems with changes of schools. They have been fortunate: for many wives and families, constant moves all over Britain can create difficulties.

The social side of a huntsman's life is quite busy, with Open Days at the kennels, terrier shows and Supporters' Club functions: they go to most things. Then there are other hunts' puppy shows to be enjoyed as guests, and their own, which inevitably involves much work but is also a tremendous occasion in the year, with many of the guests returning to their house afterwards.

Whilst an attractive house and garden with a pleasant outlook, close to the job, is an appealing prospect, there is one drawback: the smell. This was worse when Tom was a whipper-in, and busy skinning and cutting up the flesh, for his clothes also were then a perennial problem. However, his wife is not expected to clean his hunting clothes, except such items as will go in the washing machine.

One domestic duty rarely now required of huntsmen's wives used to be commonplace: taking in as lodgers young unmarried lads who came to the kennels as Whippers-in or kennelmen. Today such boys are generally expected, and indeed usually prefer, to look after themselves.

The Normington family anticipates changes in the hunting world. Perhaps it was for this reason that when Richard, the son who is most interested in horses and country life, was considering his future career, his parents influenced him against going into hunt service, encouraging him instead to enter the racing world. His mother remarked on how few of the huntsmen of their generation have sons following them into the profession. The main risk to the sport as they see it comes not from the opponents of hunting but from the erosion of the countryside.

Different attitudes to hunting in the world at large do concern Ann Normington, however. She is careful nowadays in strange company to assess other people's viewpoints before discussing her husband's work. The irresponsible behaviour of a few people is a source of anxiety which has led to the tightening of security at the kennels. When the old terrier died they decided to replace him with a Doberman. Well aware that most opposition is based on ignorance, Tom will willingly devote an evening to explaining about hunting to those prepared to consider every side. The ignorance of many opponents in the area was shown up recently when they organised a demonstration against the Drag Hounds: 'Why do you do this cruel sport? Why don't you let them kill it quickly?'

Perhaps it would surprise such people to see all the animals lovingly and skilfully cared for around the kennels. When the hound puppies are born, several soon appear in Mrs Normington's kitchen. 'If there is a large litter and the bitch hasn't a lot of milk, I help out with a bottle,' she says. In so many different ways, she provides a marvellous back-up service, primarily for her husband, but which ultimately benefits everyone connected with the Grafton Hounds.

33

THE BOOT-MAKER

Dennis Davies

As a boy, Dennis Davies was frequently in trouble – for riding. His parents, worried by the risks, would never allow him a horse. This was counter-productive, as he would catch the mountain ponies near their home in Wales to ride, and regularly 'get thrown off.' On the other hand, his father, who had retired early from his job as a fireman in the mines with chest problems, was delighted when Dennis found work in the local large footwear factory. He could never have imagined that these two sides of the boy's life would eventually combine to produce a remarkable family business.

Today, hunting men and women from all over Britain, distinguished Masters, hunt staff with many of the most eminent packs of hounds, and the cream of the eventing world, including at least three World Champions or Olympic gold medallists, have their boots made by Davies Riding Boots. This firm was started by Dennis Davies and his wife with one assistant. They have recently been joined by their daughter and son-in-law.

Dennis Davies' love of hunting began one Boxing Day with the Monmouthshire on a scooter. After he was married, he bought a horse and trailer, then started hunting with the Talybont. After two seasons, he was asked to whip in, then, three seasons later, moved to the Monmouthshire when they needed help. He whipped in there for fifteen seasons to successive huntsmen, including the first woman professional huntsman in Britain, Rachel Green. Then, with the Monmouthshire country becoming more enclosed and his own enthusiasm for jumping waning, he started hunting with the Brecon. This is a beautiful country to ride over, with virtually no jumping but wide open spaces, which suits him ideally: 'I wouldn't have much enjoyment if I couldn't see the hounds work.' He was accordingly hesitant recently about accepting an invitation for a day with the Beaufort, but at 5.45 p.m. he was still close to hounds, having jumped more fences than he had encountered in the preceding five years.

At work, he was trained as a heavy footwear manufacturer. His wife worked with him, involved latterly in quality and training. During the seventies, he dreamed of making riding boots. The Director of the factory gave him every encouragement, suggesting that he should first make himself a pair in the factory. He discussed his plan with a leading Master of Fox Hounds, who advised him that if he could produce a good quality boot at a competitive price,

Dennis Davies with some of his boots. (*James Buxton*)

the hunting world would support him. In 1977, after 27 years, he left the factory, though his wife continued part-time for a little longer.

The Master's prediction was fulfilled. Dennis Davies had just fourteen orders when he set up independently, but has never lacked work since. Next time he hunted with the Exmoor, he found six customers waiting to be measured. His reputation spread; his prices remain remarkably competitive. He found recently that his nearest rival was charging twice as much, whilst the big London makers were asking more than three times his figure. Whilst buying boots without trees is a poor economy, he is happy to alter old trees.

Boots are either wax calf or box calf. He recommends the former for hunting, sometimes the latter for eventing. With wax calf, the inside of the hide is on the outside of the boot. The suede-like feel is then waxed over when the boot is completed. With box calf, the hair side is on the outside. This is easier to keep clean, but if badly scratched it cannot be put right.

Modern leather is inferior in quality to that of thirty years ago, for tanners keep it in the pits for three months rather than a year. However, the life of boots can be greatly extended by proper care, though this is often neglected today. The first essential is to put the trees in immediately. Then Mr Davies advocates washing in cold water, drying with a paper towel and boning hard before polishing normally. It is impossible to bone polish into the leather, but the boning is important for pushing the fibres together again.

Two qualities sought for in boots are mutually incompatible. Boots, particularly in hunting conditions, will wear much better if the leather has a high fat content: some people even apply dubbin at the end of each season. However such boots will never polish to a high shine, for which a drier leather is desirable. To attain this in the past, boots were stood in the muck heap, which caused the fat content to evaporate so that they could be polished superbly, but reduced their life expectancy.

Boots are traditionally made with a single sole and a stitched in welt. However, when the stitching needs repairing new stitch holes are made so that the boot becomes progressively tighter, and reheeling and soling can cost up to £150. With Davies boots, three soles are cemented in place with a waterproof bond. Repairs are both simpler and cheaper and the boots more waterproof.

After measurements are taken (and no two people are the same, which is why the firm has to ask for a deposit), Dennis Davies and his son-in-law make the patterns and cut out the leather. The vamp is shaped in a blocking machine, a suitable calf lining selected, and the last, available in three fittings, adjusted to allow for any peculiarities such as bunions. The sewing up is mostly done by Mrs Davies, whilst their daughter takes charge of the paperwork. Excluding fitting and measuring time, each pair takes about fourteen hours. Rubber boots may be cheaper, but leather boots will probably outlast three or four rubber pairs.

An industrial estate in South Wales may seem remote from the smart premises of the traditional London bootmakers. But more and more hunting people are either finding their way there or meeting Dennis Davies at Badminton or Burghley. Perhaps the secret of his success is that 'I'm content with an average living and so long as I can have my hunting that's all that I want. At my age, every day's hunting I can get is very important to me.'

34

THE AMATEUR HUNTSMAN
Captain Brian Fanshawe

'With 150 people behind you, you always want to be going somewhere. The excitement of hunting is getting over a big area of country, ending up in the dark seven or eight miles away with people wondering how they are going to get back to their horseboxes: they love it.' Captain Brian Fanshawe is one of that select group of huntsmen, amateur or professional, who combines the pertinacity and love of venery of the true hound man with the dash and drive of foxhunting at its most popular.

When hunting the Cottesmore Hounds on their fashionable Tuesdays, he enjoys the appreciation of a big, well mounted Leicestershire field, the challenge of showing good sport in such conditions and the pleasure of riding across High Leicestershire. But equally satisfying in a different way are the days in the arable part of the country, in the company of some 20 or 30 keen foxhunters, free from pressure, concerned only with hunting hounds. The amateur huntsman, the Master who hunts hounds himself, though free of the daily kennel routine which occupies the professional, has still to take the same responsibility for managing the country as other masters.

All this Brian Fanshawe has learnt through experience, but hunting hounds is in his blood. Both his parents carried the horn. When his mother, sister to Sir Peter Farquhar, took on the South Oxfordshire during the War, Brian remembers accompanying her, first on a bicycle and later on a pony, as she hacked on to meets. He had no idea then that a whipper-in was needed: no doubt his mother felt she had a useful, if young, one.

At Sandhurst he whipped in to the Drag Hounds, and occasionally hunted them, but hounds there are seen as a fearful nuisance to proceedings. His first real opportunity came when he left the army in 1963, although it was another three and a half seasons before he hunted hounds. He ran the Warwickshire country, first on behalf of the Master, Major Cayzer, who had had a stroke, then as Master himself. Asked to estimate the cost of running the Warwickshire for the 1965 season, he assessed it at £13,555.7s.6d. A year later he was proved to be within £50 of this figure. Even so a Committee member complained of the Masters' extravagance. When asked how economies could be made, he replied that Indian tea would be cheaper than China at the Puppy Show.

Eighteen months later, when the professional huntsman was laid up in the

Captain Brian Fanshawe, MFH, with the Cottesmore Hounds. (*Jim Meads*)

season before stepping down, Brian Fanshawe hunted his first pack of fox-hounds. To him it was a natural and long anticipated development. He was already breeding the hounds, as well as exercising them regularly. That most conspicuous symbol of the huntsman, the horn, caused a few problems initially: despite constant practice, worry could lead to occasional blind spots. This was an irritation, not only because skill on the horn attracts more comment from the layman than any other aspect of hunting hounds, but also because he feels strongly that 'a horn well blown is a very stirring part of a foxhunt.' The problem was soon overcome.

In 1969 he left Warwickshire and took the Galway Blazers. Having hunted in Ireland when in the army, he regarded the country as a paradise. On a good scenting day in Galway they could cover five miles in just over fifteen minutes, jumping some thirty walls to the mile, for there were virtually no gates, with a field of seventy riding line abreast across the country. Further, the Master maintained that there was no reason at all to lose a fox in Galway, in a rideable, grass country carrying a good scent, with good visibility. He proved it. In the season before he came, hounds had killed 23 brace of foxes. In his first season he raised this to 75, in his second 85 and in his third and last 87½ brace.

There was only one problem. He was expected to hunt the country three days a week on a guarantee of just £1750 a year. Soon he returned to England, to hunt first the North Cotswold and subsequently the Cottesmore, which, alone amongst the five Shire packs, has a tradition of great amateur huntsmen.

One of the difficulties with moving from one pack to another is that the hounds so carefully bred generally remain in the same country. Brian Fanshawe has been fortunate in always being able to take representatives of his favourite female lines with him. He particularly values one such line which goes back to a bitch bought by Sir Peter Farquhar in 1925. Other successful lines go back to the Carlow Hounds and to an outstanding bitch lent him by Major Field-Marsham of the Eridge. He is currently experimenting with a cross from the Midland Hounds in Georgia.

Despite having achieved the ultimate triumph of breeding a Peterborough champion – Warwickshire Partner – he finds one hound show a year quite sufficient. He is perhaps more interested in breeding a pack as level as possible, mentally as well as physically. To achieve this, he will avoid using too many different stallion hounds in any year, and will select bitches from the same female lines, or even litter sisters. When getting to know a new pack, he will probably learn the names within a week – a feat of memory with some fifty couple – but will not look at their pedigrees until he has hunted them, to avoid prejudice.

Many huntsmen complain that the field is always on top of them and their hounds. Brian Fanshawe disagrees, asking only that they will stay quiet, and resist 'screaming about the last couple of fences they've jumped.' He is proud of his hounds and thinks it a great pity if people cannot see them, and also likes having people close enough to help with gates or sheep.

As an amateur, he is most appreciative of the part played by his kennel huntsman and first whipper-in. However, the amateur huntsman need have no anxiety about his relationship with hounds, for hounds like best the person who takes them hunting. Brian Fanshawe virtually never hits a hound, preferring to use his voice. When an old hound recently chased a deer twice in a day, he dismounted and, taking the hound by the cheek, lectured him severely until he was thoroughly ashamed of himself. When the hound was released, the rest of the pack reprimanded him more fiercely than had the Master. A lady visitor watched with interest. 'Oh Master, that was impressive,' she said. 'If you've ever got any spare time would you come to my home and do it to my 15-year-old son?'

A superb rider across country, Captain Fanshawe says only that the huntsman has more room and less poached going to contend with. He likes a horse that will approach a gate at a trot, allowing him to decide at the last moment whether to open or pop over it.

He has always been served by particularly high class terriermen, 'a must in any good foxhunting organisation.' Earth stopping, he feels, has become more of a problem with the vast increase in the badger population and the decrease in labour on farms, and it is vital that the huntsman and terrierman should work in close harmony.

Over-zealous cubhunting can cause lasting damage to coverts and hounds alike. Careful not to overdo cubhunting in any covert, he prefers to leave some places unvisited until later on. As his priority is to teach hounds to hunt away from covert, believing that the first few fields make or break most foxhunts, holding up is kept to a minimum and hounds are seldom stopped from hunting the fox. 'After all, we stop them from chasing everything else: it is a direct contradiction to tell them not to hunt the fox.'

How far behind his fox a huntsman can afford to be depends primarily on scent, which it is not always easy to assess. A fox leaving the covert at speed, looking as if he is going somewhere, is likely to give a better hunt than his more dilatory brother. Apart from the effect on scent of farming and weather conditions, and the fox himself, an important factor in Captain Fanshawe's opinion is to have hounds with 'fox-sense.' This quality, part physical, part mental, is most apparent in those packs where a rapport exists between huntsman, whipper-in and hounds, as it does with the Cottesmore. Brian Fanshawe sees his role in part as an entertainer, but 'the best way to entertain people is to hunt the fox to the best of your ability and the best of your hounds' ability.'

35

THE GIRL GROOM

Alison Whitehead

Alison Whitehead was brought up in the Lake District, where her father and brother, now huntsman of the Pennine, started hunting with the Coniston. Alison, who had always loved riding, enjoyed this but found walking the fells hard work and applied for a job looking after hunters. If this gives the impression that she is lazy, nothing could be further from the truth. Looking after hunters, which in her case have usually either been hunt horses or the Master's horses, to a high standard over a number of seasons, is incredibly hard work.

Perhaps at that stage she did not realise quite what she had taken on. Her delusions did not last long. Before hound exercise she started work at 4 a.m. It was quite a relief when cubhunting began and a 5 a.m. start was adequate. Yet she enjoyed the work and did not begrudge the fact that the early hours in autumn and late evenings after hunting, deprived her of any social life. Unlike many girls, working with show jumpers or eventers has no appeal: hunting is her interest. She has been in a number of different yards during her career, but spent seven seasons doing the York and Ainsty (South) hunt horses, including the Master's horses. She is now with the Joint Master of the West Percy, and will be whipping in to them, whilst doing her own horses.

One benefit of working for Masters has been the chance to hunt herself, a bonus which few other hunting employers are able to offer. Even if she has often been riding second horse, she has still been out with hounds. When distances were too great for more than one journey with the lorry in a day, she would frequently spend the afternoon doing the Master's first horse in the lorry after he had changed horses.

Alison's horses have always been smartly turned out: 'I think if you're going to do the job you ought to have a standard.' She likes to plait, taking ten minutes a mane using rubber bands, or half an hour if sewing, and 'can't bear seeing tails not pulled,' just as she 'hates to see a badly clipped horse.' Plaiting is particularly hectic on a frosty morning when the decision to hunt is not taken until around 9.30. The weather can also cause problems with feeding: too much food when hunting is frozen off will lead to azoturia, but a sudden thaw may mean that horses are needed, fit and ready to go, at impossibly short notice.

Alison learnt her job from the head girl she first worked under, who was

Alison Whitehead exercising a horse in West Percy country. (*James Buxton*)

competent and knowledgeable if inconsiderate. 'She showed me how to clip in three strokes then left me to get on and do it; four hours later I finished.' Today it takes her half that time. The same girl helped her build up considerable veterinary experience by trotting up unsound horses for Alison to comment on before expressing her own opinions.

Relationships with other girls in the yard can be difficult, particularly since they have frequently to share a cottage or caravan and thus have nowhere to escape from each other when tensions mount. But the competitive element sometimes leads to a higher standard throughout. Once, though, Alison left her colleague to load the horses into the lorry, and was dismayed to find when they arrived that the Field Master's horse had been left behind. Fortunately, he was able to ride the whipper-in's second horse. Other assistants too can have their drawbacks: when the Master's daughter asked to clip her own trace-clipped pony, Alison came back to find it clipped right out. The pony had to come in and join the string on exercise for the rest of the season: its rider had what she wanted, a fit pony ready to gallop. Perhaps even Alison was grateful on Saturday mornings when she took it hunting on a leading rein until the rider escaped from school.

Pressure of work in a hunt yard can be hard for staff and horses alike. One season there were two girls doing twelve horses. When the other girl became ill for three weeks, Alison was assured 'You'll manage.' For three weeks she did, helped only with the mucking out, temporarily done by the farm men. Then on occasions 'You have to patch the horses up. You knew sometimes that their legs weren't right but they weren't actually lame and they had to go. It was hard.' It is painful too to see a horse badly ridden. One whipper-in 'always used to horrify me with a great yank on the mouth and a whip down the side. I used to cringe every time I saw him do it'.

On the other hand, there is unsuspected scope for revenge. An employer is unlikely to connect a reprimand to the girl groom, apparently meekly accepted, with the fact that his horse almost bucks him off three days later. Neither horse nor girl are likely to mention the two or three extra scoops of corn it has been enjoying. There is also much fun to be had in a yard with a cheerful atmosphere. One Christmas Eve the Master's horse was led out with an enormous pair of antlers sprouting from its browband. A life with horses, hunting and the satisfaction of a job well done has much to offer.

36

THE CHAIRMAN
Lord King of Wartnaby

'If you relate being Chairman of the Belvoir to being Chairman of British Airways, British Airways is a rather more straightforward exercise.' Lord King speaks with experience: he has been Chairman of the Belvoir Hunt in Leicestershire since 1972, some years before he took on that office with British Airways. For fourteen seasons before that he was Master or Joint-Master of the Belvoir, and from 1949–58 of the Badsworth in Yorkshire.

He feels that the hunting community today expresses its views more than in the past about how things should be, but does not always remember that hunting is a privilege. The qualities which need emphasis if hunting is to be protected and preserved for the future are goodwill, sporting behaviour, responsible conduct, manners and concern towards others.

As Chairman, Lord King sees his role as one of leadership, listening to the different opinions expressed in the Hunt Committee and in the country at large, considering them and weighing them up, but eventually taking a broader view than that of any one individual. He compares the Chairman's position not only with that of the Chairman of the Board of a Company, but with that of a Member of Parliament, deciding how to vote on behalf of his constituents. But 'an excess of democracy in so far as hunting is concerned is not a good idea.'

The Belvoir is exceptional in the hunting world as the hounds do not belong, as other packs do, to the Committee, the country or to Trustees. They belong to the Duke of Rutland, and Lord King recommends names to him for possible election to the Hunt Committee. They endeavour to make it representative of the different parts of this large country. Members come up for re-election every five years. A few people, mostly newcomers, see the Committee as a power base for some other activity, and this is to be deplored.

A difficulty faced by many hunts today, particularly in countries such as the Belvoir, is the high proportion of visitors coming from outside the country to hunt there. Too many people have no idea whose land they are riding on. 'You very seldom have a problem with people who belong to the local community. If it's someone the farmers know, even if they're really fed up, it can be dealt with quite easily.'

As Chairman, such issues are generally outside Lord King's preserve, although he may occasionally be asked to go and see a particular person. He emphasises that the Masters are totally responsible for hunting the country: to be a Master is what it says and his authority must never be diluted. 'If the Chairman or Committee are dissatisfied with the manner and style in which the Masters are hunting the country, then you can tell them before they go on for another season or you can get rid of them, but the Masters have the authority and you don't want to get away from that ever.'

Lord King is a great enthusiast. His earliest ambition was to take a pack of hounds as soon as possible, and when he took the Badsworth at the age of twenty-eight, 'The local chat was "What are we doing with a wild man like that?" You learn not to be wild after a while...' He soon started hunting in Leicestershire as well as Yorkshire, eventually moving to Leicestershire, where he now farms a large acreage of land in both the Belvoir and the Quorn countries.

When he first took the Belvoir, there were twenty-eight horses in his yard: his own, those of his two Joint Masters and the hunt horses. All were immaculately turned out and done to the highest standard. Today, other pressures prevent

Lord King of Wartnaby (*right*) with the Prince of Wales and (*left*) the Duke of Rutland at the Belvoir Puppy Show. (*Jim Meads*)

him from hunting as much as formerly. But he still feels a good hunt is something special that must be protected and preserved.

Even when Lord King first took the Badsworth, the older generation was saying that hunting was not the same, there was too much wire, the country was spoilt, the future bleak. 'I thought the good old days had gone. As it happens I had the good old days.'

A generation later, he is confident that 'the country's changed, but the spirit and idea and charm of hunting is unchanged,' and has no fears for the future of the sport. He sees a greater threat from the thoughtless behaviour of hunting's adherents than in the attacks of its opponents. Opponents of hunting are often reluctant to listen to logic: in a recent television interview, Lord King was asked to comment on the cruelty involved in hunting. When he replied that another sport which he enjoys, fishing, is infinitely more cruel, that part of the interview was omitted from the programme. Yet logic has only a small part to play: the real essence of hunting is incommunicable. 'For those who don't understand hunting, no explanation is possible, for those who do understand it no explanation is necessary.'

37

THE KENNEL HUNTSMAN
Roland Sheppard

Roland Sheppard has been kennel huntsman of the Cotswold since 1967. The son of a farmer in the Quorn Monday country who hunted only occasionally in the car, Roland 'got the bug' at the age of eleven when he first had a pony, and was soon hunting regularly. He was encouraged by the hunting artist Denis Aldridge, who helped him find his first job, with the Braes of Derwent in Northumberland. After two seasons there, he moved to Lincolnshire as first whipper-in to the Brocklesby. This was an excellent education, for at the Brocklesby kennels an exceptionally high standard is maintained and, unusually, there are always sufficient staff to allow time to do things the right way.

After four seasons, he accepted the job of kennel huntsman at the Cotswold. Settling in was not easy at first, for changes in the country before his arrival had led to a somewhat strained atmosphere. Coming as he did from the Brocklesby where many farmers hunted, and most were his personal friends, it was difficult to adjust to a country with fewer hunting farmers and initially some hostility to overcome. But once everyone came to know him all such problems were resolved and he was soon immensely popular. His wife Peggy quickly became part of the local community, starting up a successful dancing school and joining the local drama group. His two daughters started at the excellent village school there, moving on to the grammar school.

Their education was the major factor in his decision to turn down the many tempting offers which were made to him to move elsewhere. Several of these would have given him the opportunity to hunt hounds regularly, a chance which he has not had with the Cotswold. For throughout his time there, successive Masters, Captain Brian Bell and Mr Tim Unwin, have hunted hounds themselves. He has thus only been able to carry the horn on, at best, one day a week, and frequently only those days when the Master was not available. This is a sacrifice which he decided to make in the interests of his family. Today, both daughters, one married, are living nearby with excellent jobs, one in insurance, the other a physiotherapist.

The Cotswold hounds themselves bear witness to their kennel huntsman's skills. They are in superb condition, hunt beautifully and won the Championship at Peterborough in 1987 and 1988.

Feeding hounds is an art at which Roland Sheppard excels. He feeds mostly raw flesh, with a little cooked meat and oatmeal. But, he says, 'It is the time in there that counts.' The shy feeders come in first so that they can eat undisturbed, then they are joined by the middle group, and finally the greedy ones are given much less time. The huntsman is always watching their condition, noting their backs across the loins, ready to restrict those putting on too much flesh and feed up any whose bones are beginning to show. Greedy ones are only fed on five days in seven; others must never miss a day.

He regards exercise as less important than feeding: 'If they're the right size they don't want a lot of exercise.' He does not believe in endless trailing round the roads in hot weather, preferring to find a stream or river and let them play in it, which is all education. On the other hand, it is important to ensure that their feet are hard. Early summer exercise is done on bicycles, moving on to horses later. Mrs Sheppard often comes out on a horse. The Cotswold is lucky in owning 100 acres, including the point-to-point course, round the kennels.

This policy also helps to prevent boredom, which can lead to fighting. Hounds can turn on one of their number, often an older one, less because he is weak than because he has become increasingly grumpy and 'the young hounds will only stand it so long'. Twice in a lifetime Roland has known such a hound to be killed; there is no pack instinct to help the underdog. A dog hound which is being picked on will sometimes benefit from being put with the bitches, or vice versa. 'It's just knowing the individual characters.' It is also necessary to notice quickly when a bitch is coming in season.

In the Cotswold kennels there are two kennelmen in addition to the kennel huntsman. The first kennelman does not ride, the second is a young man in his first job, receiving a marvellous training. The three work as a team. There is around five hours' driving to be done every day in bringing in the flesh, in addition to all the skinning. A kind local farmer mounts the second kennelman, which enables him to whip in to Roland on the days when he is hunting hounds, which is much better than having an amateur who does not know the names of the hounds. Carrying the horn on occasional days only is never easy, for hounds are used to being turned to the Master by Roland, who has accordingly to be exceptionally quiet and careful in the way he handles them.

Those walking puppies are advised not to take them out a great deal, but to encourage them to stay close to home. Puppies should be taught their names, handled as much as possible, shut in when necessary and tied up occasionally. They should also be taught to lead, for on their return they will be coupled to an older hound on exercise. Once they start wanting to hunt it is time for them to return to kennels.

The kennel huntsman has to do some veterinary work, washing wounds with salt water, giving antibiotic injections, occasionally stitching, or putting vegetable oil on a jagged wound to encourage the others to lick it. The whole pack must also be wormed twice a year.

Whilst the breeding is done by the Master, the kennel huntsman's advice is

Roland Sheppard with Cotswold Grappler '85, the hunt's first Peterborough Champion. (*Jim Meads*)

sought. As well as the more conventional bloodlines, the Fell hound Blencathra Glider has been used with considerable success. Showing hounds is hard work, both in the preparation and on the day. Peterborough involves seven hours driving in the lorry in addition to the strain of the show itself, dressed in heavy hunting clothes in July. In such circumstances momentary inattention by the kennelman in the ring may lead to a sharp rebuke. Some hounds also are much easier to show than others; the two champions, Grappler and Grocer, were naturals, worthy ambassadors of their kennel huntsman's skill.

38

THE HUNTING TAILOR
John Green of 'Frank Hall'

'We had been making for the Brocklesby since the late 1920s. They used to have about seven in scarlet, the huntsman, two whips, their three second horsemen and the Master's second horseman. They even used to buy clothes for the earth-stoppers. In those days kennel coats were tailor made. And there was a lot more indoor livery. Butlers and footmen had coats and waistcoats, that sort of thing.'

Today, hunting men and women from every part of Britain come to Frank Hall of Market Harborough to be measured by Mr Green or his colleague Mr Ripley for their hunting coats and breeches. Mr Green was himself brought up in a family firm started by his great grandfather in 1870 close to the Pytchley kennels in Brixworth, about ten miles away. At one time there were over twenty tailors, but no tailoresses, employed in the business. Sadly his father died whilst he was still a child, in 1935. Then the War came, the indoor servant trade disappeared completely, and there were no longer establishments where half a dozen grooms would each have a new stable suit made for them every year: 'The suits were made of old fashioned stable tweed, which was really a heavy weight whipcord: it's not been made for twenty-five years.' John Green's efforts to rebuild the family firm as soon as he was old enough to make the attempt were heroic but inevitably doomed.

However, as one tailor to another, he did have occasional dealings with the business of Frank Hall. Mr Hall had three sons, but his intended successor had been killed in the War, another was abroad and the third, Robert, had other interests. When Frank Hall advertised in the *Tailor and Cutter* for an assistant, he indicated that he was looking for a man of thirty-five with considerable experience, so the young man did not bother to apply. But Robert Hall contacted him and eventually he was asked to join the firm.

Whilst the Hall family made him most welcome, and he brought some of his own customers with him, matters moved rather more slowly with Mr Hall's long standing clientele. 'You had to be here ten years before a good many customers would accept you. It's such a personal business. Mr Ripley has been here since 1961. Now anybody is prepared to see him as well as myself, but for the first five or ten years they didn't want to see him the same as originally they didn't want to see me, they always wanted to see Mr Hall.'

Mr Green (*left*) and Mr Ripley of Frank Hall of Market Harborough.
(*Andrew Carpenter*)

Today Mr Green and Mr Ripley do all the cutting and fitting. 'He cuts the gents' coats and suits. I cut ladies' hunting coats and all the breeches. The problem for years has been staff. We're definitely a dying race. The London firms are nowhere near as big as they used to be. They share workshops and staff. Here unless we train them ourselves we've got nobody else to fall back on.' The making up of the clothes is done in two workshops on the spot, and there are also 'various outworkers: one or two tailoresses who have retired. The snag is they don't pass their skill on to anybody else.'

Another difficulty is that, although they buy the best quality materials available, 'I'm sorry to say they don't wear as well as they used to. They cost considerably more . . .' Whereas coats made in the immediate post War period are 'tough and hard and strong, but in this sort of business we don't like somebody coming along and saying "I've only had this coat for ten years and it's got a hole in it," but it does happen.'

Inflation, particularly in such a labour-intensive trade, means that people occasionally complain that they are paying more for minor alterations than the coat cost when new. 'Our customers think prices are high; they frighten us sometimes, but we don't charge prices that the West End does: we haven't got the West End's overheads.' Sometimes a new client, being given a quotation, will comment 'That's very reasonable', whilst 'the old ones go through the roof.' High costs also mean that 'you cannot afford to have a well-paid deputy.' Mr Green has one daughter, an accountant, and Mr Ripley has three daughters, but none are interested in the business.

When Frank Hall was alive, he was regularly making a wider range of clothes, side saddle habits, children's riding clothes, coats and skirts for women and teenage girls, brown breeches with black or dark grey coats for stud grooms and coat and breeches alike in dark grey for ordinary grooms. 'Sir Evelyn Fanshawe was one of the last private people who bought their grooms' clothes. He was a very good friend to us.' Many will remember Sir Evelyn as one of the best turned out men to cross Leicestershire in the last twenty years.

Today, Mr Green and Mr Ripley are almost exclusively concerned with hunting coats and breeches and men's suits. But their clientele includes many of the most famous names in the hunting world and hunt staff from countries all over Britain. They also hold a Royal Warrant from the Prince of Wales, for the famous blue Windsor coat is made in Market Harborough. One of the original reasons for its adoption was to obviate the need to select a particular hunt button, as would have been necessary if the Prince of Wales were hunting in scarlet.

Hunt buttons can be a source of contention. Whilst Mr Green feels that 'little points of etiquette are overlooked today', his guiding influence is sometimes needed. 'We try to ensure nobody wears a hunt button who is not entitled to, and always advise people to take things slowly and become a full hunting person before trying to go out in a scarlet swallowtail, shall we say.' A problem did arise many years ago when ladies' hunting coats in the now popular style with two buttons at the back first came in. One of the earliest owners of such a coat was the daughter of an eminent Master who, at his instigation, had it made with four buttons at the front, as is correct for Masters. A friend then ordered a coat for herself, saying that she wanted it exactly the same. She was less pleased with the result when a punctilious Hunt Secretary demanded that she should chop off the bottom button. Such coats are now invariably made with three buttons, except for Masters.

Mr Green may see himself as a member of a dying race, and certainly during his lifetime the trade has changed so immeasurably that, where Market Harborough once boasted two such firms and nearby Brixworth a third, he is now left with few rivals outside London. He has done more than survive: he has succeeded, by offering a high standard of service as well as of workmanship, in winning himself a unique place in the world of hunting.

39

THE MASTER OF A FAMILY PACK

Vyvyan Eames

V yvyan Eames first hunted the Cotley Hounds at the age of fifteen. It cannot, however, be said that he first carried the horn on that date. As his younger brother Edward was more proficient on that instrument than he, Edward accompanied him, blowing the horn to the young huntsman's orders, holding his horse when asked and otherwise helping. Their father, Lt Col R. F. P. Eames, the Master, tactfully stayed in the background. With a small, invited field and 8 or 9 couple of hounds, the day was a success. When the Master inspected hounds in kennel that evening, he informed his sons that they had killed a fox. The fox was picked up next day – hounds had not broken it up – and the present Master still has the brush.

The Cotley Hounds were founded in 1797 by Mr T. Deane. He was succeeded 58 years later by his son-in-law Mr T. P. Eames. Ever since, a member of the Eames family has been in the Mastership. The hounds, in common only with their neighbours the Axe Vale, hunt foxes and are recognised by the MFHA, but are entered in the Harrier Stud Book. Green coats are worn by the honorary whippers-in, of whom there are eight, representing other members of the Eames family and two generations each of the Legg and Burrough families (who are themselves intermarried.) The Master hunts hounds on Wednesdays and Saturdays. The country lies almost equally in Devon, Somerset and Dorset, between Chard, Honiton, Axminster and the sea.

Hunt finances must be the envy of every other hunt in Britain. There is a substantial bank balance which is not drawn upon, subscriptions are just £100 and farmers are not expected to subscribe, merely paying, in common with subscribers, £4 or £5 in field money per day. Some £10,000 is raised annually during the first week-end in May, when both the Hunt Ball and the point-to-point are held at the Master's home.

It is possible to contain costs to this level because the Master and the whippers-in all mount themselves at their own expense. The only hunt employee is David Gaylard, the kennel huntsman, who does not come out hunting unless there happens to be a spare horse available. Everything possible is done on a voluntary basis. At the point-to-point, for example, voluntary help cuts the birch, builds the fences, operates the tote and even runs the bar on the day. The course is then hired out to two adjacent hunts at an index-linked rent.

Vyvyan Eames, MFH (*mounted*) with his late father Lt Col R. F. P. Eames Eames, MFH, and the Cotley Hounds at Cotley. (*D. J. Wheadon, Chard*)

A true cross section of the local community hunts, though those living outside the country are rarely accepted. The Field Master is the local bank manager, and three hunting nurses probably saved the Master's life recently following a bad fall. The Master commented that an outsider wishing to build a house in the country could find in the hunting field every expert he would require, surveyor, architect, solicitor, plumber, electrician, builder, decorator and even someone to empty the septic tank!

He might have rather more difficulty in finding the land. Most farms have been in the same families for generations, and these families tend to be land hungry, buying up any land which does come on to the market. The Master rarely spends time visiting farmers as he has known them all his life. His brother Edward and Edward's wife run a big skittle league with 500 members for the hunt. This involves most of the farmers, is immensely popular and provides an excellent opportunity for Master, farmers and hunting people to meet.

There are some remarkable characters in the country, all of whom have given the present Master the same loyal support which they gave his father. One of the whippers-in, Bob Burrough, is 84 and still hunts one day a week. The terriers are worked by Norman Bartlett who, in his seventies, continues to hunt the Culmstock Mink (formerly Otter) Hounds. He has recently married for the first time, with Vyvyan Eames as his Best Man. When he sold his farm to a property developer, after exchanging contracts in the solicitor's office, he came out with the Cotley and was seen disappearing into a large earth behind a terrier with the cheque for 10% of the price of the farm in his back trouser pocket.

The Cotley Hounds are West Country Harriers, extremely attractive, almost white hounds, closer to harriers than foxhounds, though rather larger than the conventional harrier. They hunt with a tremendous cry. The late Colonel Eames introduced a most successful cross with the College Valley. Recently, in an effort to reduce the size somewhat, College Valley blood has not been used, but a South Poole dog has been. The Cotley are too large to be shown at Peterborough, but David Gaylard, the kennel huntsman, has shown them very successfully at Honiton Hound Show, maintaining a long sequence of Championship wins. He and the Master do the breeding together: 'A hound has to look nice and hunt well too for us to breed from it.'

Before the War, they hunted both hare and fox, but the last hare was killed in 1938, the year before Colonel Eames became Master. He had first worn a green coat at the age of nine when he was known as the 'sixth whip'. Whilst hunting the Trinity Foot Beagles at Cambridge, he decided that harriers were too large to hunt hares. Despite being handicapped with a stiff leg following a war wound, Colonel Eames was an outstanding huntsman, handling his hounds with a remarkable quiet, unruffled skill. He remained Joint Master with his son until his death in 1987.

His son Vyvyan preferred rugger to the beagles whilst at school at Radley, but enjoyed both hunting and, later, point-to-pointing. Despite his claim that he generally fell off, he won a number of Members' races and an occasional Open race. He has been a National Hunt steward at Taunton for some years, as well as being Chairman of the West of England Hound Show at Honiton and Treasurer of the local Riding for the Disabled Association. After qualifying as a Chartered Accountant, he returned home to run the estate, and now has some 900 acres in hand which he farms himself without a manager. There is a small family shoot at Cotley, with 350 birds being put down annually, some 50% of which are shot, even though hounds draw through all the coverts at the Opening Meet, always finding, and foxes are never interfered with.

Vyvyan Eames joined his father in the Mastership in 1972 and gradually took over hunting hounds. Colonel Eames proved an exemplary father, never interfering, but always available to advise if asked. The hunt remains a family concern: Mrs Eames undertakes all the traditional commitments of the Master's wife and many more besides, from running the Hunt Ball to doing some of the horses, and both daughter Mary and son Tom love their hunting. The Cotley Hounds look secure for at least another generation.

40

THE MOTORBIKE FOLLOWER

Baz Hughes

'The fun we've had. Anybody's that anti-hunting, if they knew what they were missing...' His attitude will be shared by many in the Wynnstay country, where Baz Hughes has taken on the role of resident comic. He says of those who are paid to come out into the country and demonstrate against hunting: 'A good lunch and cash – if it was a non-hunting day I'd go myself!'

He started hunting regularly in his late teens when he met Paul Connolly, the terrier man, at the motor engineers where he worked. Baz had always liked working dogs and was soon being initiated into the world of terriers and of foxhounds. He was in good hands: 'Paul give me the groundwork for everything, and if you did happen to make a mistake you just got your ear bent, if your were extremely lucky. Paul and Steven are great believers that the more people you get involved, the less ignorance about the sport there'll be, and the better the sport will become for it. I've served me time but I'm still the lad, although I've been at it twenty years. It's an honour to be involved with a bloke like that.'

Steven Creer, another Wynnstay stalwart, introduced him to the wider world of hunting, taking him to visit other packs, the Fell packs, Exmoor, the Quorn, Cheshire and a pack of otterhounds in Ireland. The latter pack was in the habit of receiving drafts of hounds from English packs, and soon Baz started keeping such hounds in his own kennels for the weeks during which they were awaiting shipment to Ireland. On one occasion, while out exercising, three and a half couple, together with his own terrier and springer spaniel, picked up the line of a fox. They were hunting beautifully with a lovely cry, but Baz raced back home for a hunting horn then ran to them. 'I was in a blind panic. I could hardly breathe, never mind blow the trumpet.' He waited for them to check and, with the aid of a hind quarter of beef, they were soon securely back in kennels once more. It was some time before people stopped asking him about the private pack they had heard was starting up.

He was not usually involved in the transport of his charges to Ireland, but on one occasion he, Steven and a third friend were planning to take some hounds over in a van, but the friend insisted on using his own almost new Ford Escort. The three men, with their suitcases on the roof rack, and five and a half couple of hounds were fitted in somewhere, and they even found a kennel on the boat before retiring to the bar. Soon the music on the boat was backed by music of another sort, resounding across the Irish Sea.

Baz has walked a number of hound puppies, and finds this adds a new dimension to the sport. 'Each individual hound, they're all characters, but if you walk one and you know maybe their litter sister and brother, or even the litter sister's sons and daughters, it's not very long before you get to know a good part of the kennel, and that's the enjoyment, who's took it up, and who's found it . . . then you take a special interest. I love the hound work, you see. I love horses but I love the hound more and I get a lot of pleasure out of seeing them.'

The way in which he usually sees hounds is on a motorbike. He started using this means of transport when helping with the earth stopping, for there was a lot to be done, and much time could be saved in this way. During a day's hunting, though, he normally stays on the public roads, though if he has something important to communicate, 'you nip through the odd time. There's never any

Baz Hughes celebrating a good hunt with the Wynnstay. (*Jim Meads*)

trouble. The most trouble is with the (other) lads thrusting on, when there is a chance of heading something, but nine times out of ten there are about forty cars there but it's always the bike that gets the blame.' There are times when a bike can help the huntsman on a day's hunting, staying in touch with hounds if the horses are wired up or blown, or reaching a main road in front of hounds. He feels also that only four stroke bikes should be used, as these emit virtually no exhaust fumes. He also does his best to educate newcomers: 'It's our necks that are on the line so they've got to be (educated). I mean, roaring about and shouting and bawling and thinking every fox is the hunted fox is understandable when you first start, but . . .' It is certainly not the way in which Baz approaches his hunting.

Bill Lander, erstwhile professional huntsman of the Wynnstay and a great ambassador for the sport, talked Baz into the horse side of hunting, and he would ride to hounds every day if he could afford to, preferring a horse to a bike whenever the chance arises. On his first day mounted, dressed in borrowed clothes, there was a good hunt across the cream of the country and, on a first-rate performer following a noted hard rider, his confidence increased at every fence, riding with what he describes as the 'no guidance from above approach'. Less successful was the day when Bill sent him on round a covert, over a tiger trap with a strand of wire underneath it. The horse shied, he fell off, hung on to the horse with one arm, but got the other arm through the bars of the tiger trap hooked on to the wire. He finished the day with his sleeve pinned to his coat.

His wife, Roz, goes superbly across a country, whether riding side-saddle or astride. She has hunted all her life in the country, but as they do not at present have a horse, she has recently passed her motorbike test. For a Supporters' Club pantomime, Roz helped him to make a magnificent ostrich outfit for a Bernie Clifton-type act. It has been such a success that people have hired it on several occasions since.

He had not been hunting long before he found that 'if you missed a day's hunting you felt sick. Work went by the wayside.' He is now a self-employed motor mechanic. Much of his work is for hunting people, and he works the hours which fit in with hunting.

Recent visits by the Wynnstay hounds to other countries, and, in return, by other packs to their country, have given him much pleasure. No doubt the visitors also have enjoyed themselves, for there is very little plough in this country on the Welsh borders, and much work has been done in opening it up. To Baz, 'the nicest part of these visits is coming home: it makes you really appreciate what you've got.' He is most appreciative of the different contributions made by others to hunting, and feels that the first thing newcomers ought to learn is 'respect for the people who put all the big money into the sport.' As for himself, 'If I can make somebody laugh, I'm happy, because hunting should be fun.'

41

THE PROFESSIONAL WHIPPER-IN
Debbie Murphy

Debbie Murphy was born at Gosport, where her father was serving in the navy, and spent part of her childhood in Malta and in Singapore. She rode other people's ponies when the opportunity arose, but her parents were horrified when she suggested that she should work with horses on leaving school. Her first job almost persuaded her that she would indeed have fared better as a secretary; she was paid just £3 a week to work at a riding school, and found herself dependent on food parcels sent by her mother.

After three months she was offered a job by Bob Buswell, the retired professional huntsman, who was then running a private boarding kennels and hunting with the Hambledon. He first introduced her to the sport where she has made her career. Her next move was to Mr Goschen's Hunt yard, where she first worked with the horses, but was subsequently offered the chance to whip in. Her sex caused no problems, for the pack had a tradition of girl whippers-in. She found the huntsman, Ted Rafton, most patient, and still regards his advice always to stay in close touch with hounds as a golden rule of whipping in. At that time she was criticised for not using her voice sufficiently, but she has now overcome this.

After leaving Mr Goschen's Hounds, she spent a year in a racing yard, but found the turnover of horses there too fast and impersonal. Next, she spent three seasons in Yorkshire with the Master of the Goathland, before coming to Dumfriesshire in 1984. She had been going to work for one of the joint Masters, but as there was a vacancy in the kennel yard at this time she went there instead. Peter Reed, who was then kennel huntsman as the Master, Sir Rupert Buchanan-Jardine, hunted hounds himself, noticed her watching somewhat wistfully whenever he walked out hounds, accompanied by one of the kennelmen, and encouraged her to help with hounds. When she brought out a second horse, she would also give some assistance with the whipping in in the hunting field. In 1987 Sir Rupert gave up hunting hounds. Peter Reed became professional huntsman and Debbie was officially appointed First Whipper-In, and wore a red coat.

Nevertheless, she continues to do the four hunt horses as well as working in kennels. They have had the same four horses for some seasons, including a little thoroughbred mare of which she is particularly fond. The Dumfriesshire is a

Debbie Murphy with the Dumfriesshire Hounds in kennels. (*Meriel Buxton*)

marvellous riding country, nearly all grass and stone walls, with a large, hard riding field. Debbie's only complaint about it is that she cannot tell where the bogs are, and maintains that, whilst Peter Reed's horses seem to know, hers do not!

Her first love, though, is for hounds, and particularly these magnificent big black and tan hounds: 'I couldn't imagine going back to another ordinary pack now. You get bitten by the bug of these hounds.' For they are different in temperament as well as appearance from other foxhounds. Debbie recalls the visit of another pack to the kennels: 'I couldn't get over how well-controlled these other hounds were. They trotted along the road and stayed together. When we go hound exercising it's fraught with dangers: if there's a fox about, that's it – they just go.' Yet in practice she and Peter Reed control them with conspicuous success. 'They seem to respond to me,' Debbie says simply. Jimmy Gutch, who has followed these hounds for many years, explains: 'She's got that understanding with them. They'll go with her. They won't go with everyone, of course. It's a tremendous gift to have to start off with.'

Whilst their colour makes the Dumfriesshire hounds much more difficult than an ordinary pack of foxhounds for the outsider to distinguish, for Debbie they are very much individuals. As a result, she admits guiltily to having favourites amongst them: 'I know you shouldn't, but there are some that you adore'. One such is Rochdale, whom she walked, keeping him as a puppy in her own bedsitting room until he himself made it plain that he wished to rejoin the pack. Rochdale's sire Rockwood once could not be found after an exceptionally windy day's hunting. Five days later, hounds were meeting six miles away. Rockwood appeared at the meet, hunted all day and returned safely to kennels with them that night.

The world-wide popularity of the Dumfriesshire Hounds means that any surplus hounds are always in demand somewhere, often abroad. Except on the rare occasions when a hound commits the one unforgivable sin of sheep worrying, there will always be a home for it. An important aspect of Debbie's work in the field is to anticipate and prevent any problems with sheep. An aggressive old tup is kept in a paddock at the kennels to teach the young hounds, before they are entered, how sheep should be treated. Out hunting, sheep are just one of the hazards: main roads and railways present further potential dangers. As whipper-in, 'You've just got to keep your wits about you all the time. There's no going to sleep.' Debbie appreciates the help Peter Reed gives her and is fortunate in having a competent amateur whipper-in to assist her.

She does not usually have to do the skinning, except in emergencies, as two kennelmen are employed, but in the summer she does a large part of the bringing in of flesh. She enjoys this, for it gives her the chance to see the country from a different angle, noticing any changes which have occurred during the summer, and to get to know the farmers whilst giving them a service which they appreciate. She does not, however, enjoy dealing with any meat with maggots in. Although Mrs Goschen was originally concerned that she would not be strong enough for the work, this has never proved a problem.

The small number of 'male chauvinist pigs' whom she has encountered have also been proved wrong: they suggested that she 'couldn't do a man's job, but I do.'

42

THE PHOTOGRAPHER
Jim Meads

By the start of his forty-first season as a hunting photographer, Jim Meads had been out with three hundred and ninety-one different packs of hounds. Wherever in the world there is hunting, Jim Meads is known and liked. The sight of his familiar figure at the meet, camera in hand, sends a ripple of excitement through the field: anticipation as to whose likeness will shortly feature in *Horse and Hound*, perhaps relief or regret over an earlier decision to wear the best new coat, or to leave the horse unplaited, but never the anxiety or mistrust accorded to so many denizens of the press. For Jim Meads inspires total confidence. His photographs are superb. He will never take advantage of an unfortunate moment: his pictures may occasionally amuse but they are never unkind. As well as having tact, discretion and common sense, he understands hunting. He can be counted on never to frighten a horse, never to be in anybody's way, never to head a fox.

Hounds at the meet, covert side or trotting down the road are a popular subject for photography, and every competitive rider is sent countless proofs of their horse jumping a fence. But action photographs of hunting are rare, for they can seldom be taken except by a running photographer such as Jim Meads. He is always up with hounds on his feet, difficult enough without the added impediment of the camera and the need to anticipate precisely which way hounds will run and the field will go. 'I'm the only one who's ever done it like that; it's the only way to get pictures,' he says. He has always kept fit. In summer until recently he played cricket on four days a week. As a member of David Nicholson's National Hunt team, of which the Queen Mother is patron, he has taken part in matches at Lord's and in Barbados.

Jim's father Frank was a staff photographer on *Country Life* up to the War, taking photographs of hunting in winter and gardens in summer. It was a relatively easy life: he would cover one day's hunting in a week where his son will now cover perhaps four. When Jim first joined his father on coming out of the Royal Air Force in 1950, 'it was a typical family concern: I took the pictures and he took the money!' He describes his early experience with the camera as 'Hit and miss: I learnt by my own mistakes and didn't make them twice, hopefully. I don't know anything about the theory of it at all. It would be no good me trying to teach someone else; if it looks right I take it.' He has a

Photographer Jim Meads with the David Davies hounds and their huntsman
David Jones. (*Jim Meads*)

remarkable eye to achieve the results he does, for he works fast, unlike many
photographers, and regards this as essential: 'By the time they get things
organised the picture's gone.' But he does not work on the system of taking a
large number of photographs and afterwards selecting the best. 'I take one to get
one,' he says.

Jim Meads was brought up in the Enfield Chace country, where he was
blooded in 1936. He belonged to the Pony Club, in company with Raymond
Brooks-Ward and Tom Hudson, and was taught to ride by the redoubtable
Miss Joan Middleton, though the need to earn his living caused him to give up
riding. For the first five years he travelled everywhere by motorbike, unable to
afford a car. For eighteen years he lived on the borders of the Grafton and

Bicester countries, a central position which made his constant travelling relatively easy. But, despite the additional travelling, he has no regrets about his decision to move to the Welsh mountains. 'It's worth it to live where I do in the David Davies country.'

He numbers hunt servants throughout Britain and Ireland amongst his closest friends. His guests at a recent party included some of the top professional huntsmen from every corner of the British Isles. This special relationship helps in his work, for 'they know me and can trust me not to be in the way when hounds run.'

His work can be dangerous. He was once kicked in the face by a horse with the Tanatside, and woke up in Welshpool Hospital, where 'apparently I wouldn't let go of my camera.' His first priority was to return and take more pictures to ensure that he did not lose his nerve. Another hazard is being jumped on. From the landing side of a big drop fence in Leicestershire, it is impossible for him to see or be seen, and, whilst he has one eye glued to the viewfinder on the camera, the other is constantly watching out.

Jim Meads has remained freelance throughout his career, although all his work is now commissioned, mostly by *Horse and Hound* or *The Field*. He is now in demand all over the world, and has travelled frequently to America, Canada, Australia and France. The day in 1962 when he was first offered work in Ireland and 'I thought I'd really arrived' seems a very long time ago.

Ever the professional, he takes as much trouble over ensuring that his captions are correct as he takes over the picture itself. He retains his own energetic style of working even away from the hunting field. If covering a three day event, in Britain or abroad, he will run round the course, rarely failing to picture every horse at a different fence.

His collection of hunting pictures is unique, including as it does those taken by his father in the thirties. It is a remarkable historical record, from the great hunting figures of those days to such modern personalities as the Prince of Wales, for whom Jim Meads has tremendous admiration. Some reflect the changing face of the country. Where Frank Meads once photographed hounds meeting outside a large house, a bus garage now stands in Potters Bar High Street, close to the M25. Other changes in hunting can bring unexpected benefits. Arable land is now put down to winter wheat before the season starts. Horses find this as heavy to cross as plough, and are less welcome on it. But for hounds, and for the running photographer, drilled land can be crossed as easily as grass.

Jim Meads makes no attempt to look into a crystal ball, and neither of his sons has followed him into his profession, their sporting interests being concentrated respectively on cricket and on fishing. Yet his philosophy is reflected in the titles of his books. His father originally published *They Meet at Eleven*. Jim followed this with *They Still Meet at Eleven*. He is now bringing out *They Will Always Meet at Eleven*.